The Multi-Disciplinary Instructional Designer

The Multi-Disciplinary Instructional Designer explores how the instructional design and development process can be energized and deepened through principles gleaned from other fields of academic study. Despite their shared academic preparation and theoretical foundations, many instructional designers come to the profession also bearing formative knowledge from a diverse range of other subject areas, career tracks, creative practices, or intellectual pursuits. Their training, however, typically does not prepare them to leverage these specializations into the creation of more effective educational experiences and materials. This first-of-its-kind book guides instructional designers to apply key concepts, strategies, and lessons learned from a variety of disciplines – spanning the social sciences, arts and humanities, and STEM – to their practice. Chapters replete with example scenarios, reflection activities, and field-tested strategies provide an expansive yet actionable reframing of the profession's potential. By seeking inspiration across disciplines and from the world at large, instructional designers will emerge with robust and revitalized toolkits, ready to enrich their approach to teaching and learning.

Chris Gamrat is Assistant Teaching Professor in the College of Information Sciences and Technology at the Pennsylvania State University, USA.

Megan Kohler is Learning Designer and Lecturer in the John A. Dutton e-Education Institute at The Pennsylvania State University, USA.

The Multi-Disciplinary Instructional Designer

Integrating Specialized Skills into Design Toolkits

**EDITED BY
CHRIS GAMRAT
AND MEGAN KOHLER**

NEW YORK AND LONDON

Designed cover image: © Getty Images

First published 2023
by Routledge
605 Third Avenue, New York, NY 10158

and by Routledge
4 Park Square, Milton Park, Abingdon, Oxon, OX14 4RN

Routledge is an imprint of the Taylor & Francis Group, an informa business

© 2023 selection and editorial matter, Chris Gamrat and Megan Kohler;
individual chapters, the contributors

The right of Chris Gamrat and Megan Kohler to be identified as the authors
of the editorial material, and of the authors for their individual chapters,
has been asserted in accordance with sections 77 and 78 of the Copyright,
Designs and Patents Act 1988.

All rights reserved. No part of this book may be reprinted or reproduced or
utilised in any form or by any electronic, mechanical, or other means, now
known or hereafter invented, including photocopying and recording, or in
any information storage or retrieval system, without permission in writing
from the publishers.

Trademark notice: Product or corporate names may be trademarks or
registered trademarks, and are used only for identification and explanation
without intent to infringe.

ISBN: 978-1-032-21434-4 (hbk)
ISBN: 978-1-032-20205-1 (pbk)
ISBN: 978-1-003-26841-3 (ebk)

DOI: 10.4324/9781003268413

Typeset in Avenir & Dante
by Apex CoVantage, LLC

To my family and friends, thank you for your support and encouragement. Your faith in me has helped me to become a better person.

To my colleagues past and present, your passion for education has continued to inspire me to learn more. I am lucky to have worked with you, and I have tremendously valued our conversations.

Chris Gamrat

I'm blessed to have many kind and caring people in my life who have given me unwavering support as I have pursued many professional goals. I would like to dedicate this book to those individuals.

My husband, Nate. Thank you for your continual support, encouragement, and love.

My beautiful children, Shiloh and Alex. You have enriched my life in ways I never thought possible. I am blessed to have you in my life.

My friend, Christine. You gave me the courage to pursue my dreams. Thank you for believing in me, challenging me, and encouraging me.

Megan Kohler

Contents

List of Contributing Authors	*ix*
Foreword	*xi*
Lloyd Rieber	
Preface	*xiv*

1 A Closer Look at Instructional Design   1
    Carl S. Moore and Julaine Fowlin

2 A Consultative Mindset: Aligning Strategic Learning
    Initiatives Using Marketing-Based Approaches   15
    Robyn A. Defelice

3 Out of the Frying Pan, Into the Fire: The Unintended
    (and Amazing) Consequences of Risk-Taking in the Practice
    of Instructional Design   35
    Paul F. Desmarais

4 Critical Theory for Critical Work: Feminist Approaches to
    Instructional Design   51
    Jaclyn Dudek

5 A Tale of Two English Teachers: Instructional Design
    Lessons Learned From the Classroom   67
    Erica C. Fleming and Sharon Tjaden-Glass

viii Contents

6 Building Resilient Courses: How Crisis Management
Can Inform Instructional Design 83
Chris Gamrat, Edward J. Glantz, and Lisa Lenze

7 Always on Stage: Acting and Improv Skills for Creating
More Collaborative Design Dynamics 103
Penny Ralston-Berg and Megan Kohler

8 Designing Therapeutic Landscapes for Learners: What
a Critical Health Geography Approach Can Add to the Field
of Instructional Design 126
Michelle Deborah Majeed

9 STEM and Instructional Design: A Discussion of STEM
Identity Soft Skills in the Instructional Design Field 142
Blair Stamper

10 Lessons From the Barre: The Intersection Between Dance
and Dynamic Instructional Design Decision-Making 159
Jill E. Stefaniak

11 Instructional Design as Communication: Insights From
the Field of Journalism 178
Richard E. West

Index *195*

Contributing Authors

Robyn A. Defelice, Ph.D., is an independent learning strategist and consultant

Paul F. Desmarais, M.ET., is the managing partner at OLIDA Learning.

Jaclyn Dudek, Ph.D., is an assistant professor & assistant researcher in the Department of Curriculum and Teaching, School of Education and Human Systems & The Center for Certification and Competency-based Education at the University of Kansas.

Erica C. Fleming, M.A., is the assistant director of teaching and learning in the College of Information Sciences & Technology at The Pennsylvania State University.

Julaine Fowlin, Ph.D., is the assistant director for instructional design in the Center for Teaching at Vanderbilt University.

Chris Gamrat Ph.D., is an assistant teaching professor in the College of Information Sciences & Technology at The Pennsylvania State University.

Edward J. Glantz, Ph.D., is a teaching professor in the College of Information Sciences & Technology at The Pennsylvania State University.

Megan Kohler, M.S.I.T., is a learning designer and lecturer in the College of Earth and Mineral Sciences at The Pennsylvania State University.

Lisa Lenze, Ph.D., is the director of teaching, learning, & assessment in the College of Information Sciences & Technology at The Pennsylvania State University..

x Contributing Authors

Michelle Deborah Majeed, M.A., is an instructional designer in the Faculty & Curriculum Development Centre (FCDC) at OCAD University.

Carl S. Moore, Ph.D., is the vice president for teaching and learning at Howard Community College.

Penny Ralston-Berg, M.S., is a senior instructional designer with the World Campus at The Pennsylvania State University.

Blair Stamper, M.A., is an instructional designer at The University of North Carolina at Charlotte.

Jill E. Stefaniak, Ph.D., is an associate professor at University of Georgia.

Sharon Tjaden-Glass, M.A., is an instructional media designer at Sinclair Community College.

Richard E. West, Ph.D., is a professor at Brigham Young University.

Foreword

I have long been fascinated with the stories people tell about how they found out about and then pursued a career in the field of learning, design, and technology. My fascination stems from the fact that few people tell the same story. Most tell a tale that is usually more about falling into this career unexpectedly rather than the result of some systematic search or lifelong ambition. And let's be honest, when you were asked in fifth grade what you wanted to be when you grew up, you didn't say instructional designer or project manager.

This book is long overdue. It is time, finally, to tell the unique stories of at least a handful of our most creative and successful learning design and technology (LDT) professionals. As you read these stories, be sure to remember always that your story is another worth telling. It probably won't resemble anything you find in the chapters that follow, but that's exactly the point of this book.

The start of my own story is actually more typical of many because I began my career in education from the start. I was an elementary school teacher who wanted to further my education in an area related to technology in education. But the rest of my story is again unlike anyone else's. First, I was an elementary school teacher in New Mexico, which was very unusual because I was living in my hometown of Pittsburgh at the time I was offered the job. But even getting to the point of being offered a teaching job was not something I could have predicted just a few years before. I began my college career studying engineering, but soon discovered that was a poor career path for me. Then, like many undergraduates, I struggled to find my niche and eventually discovered my interest in working with children through summer jobs and experiences. And that led me to teaching. And so in January 1980, my

xii Foreword

family and I moved to New Mexico for my first teaching job at a small rural elementary school in Bluewater, New Mexico (population then and now of about 500).

When you first start teaching, everything is new to you – how to effectively manage a classroom, how to work with parents, how to do lunchroom or bus duty, how to try to teach well day after day, and so on, and so on. But to my great fortune, this school had a very progressive principal, Jerry Morris, and he was determined to have his school include the newly emerging innovation known as the Apple computer. But to me the Apple computer was just yet another new thing for me to learn. I didn't notice it at the time, but apparently the other teachers were quite resistant to having anything to do with these few computers tucked away in the back corner of the school library. I can now see how Mr. Morris reinforced and supported my meager efforts because, well, I was actually doing something meaningful with them. I look back at what a marvelous and serendipitous intersection of roads I found myself standing in the middle of in the early 1980s. I happened to land in a place where I was learning how to teach, how to use technology in my teaching, and how to work with people with cultural backgrounds much different from my own. It's also good to remember that back then there were no rules or district policies yet invented about how to use a computer in the classroom, so I was free to try all sorts of things, including having my students learn Seymour Paper's LOGO programming language and me learning to program education games for the Apple computer in partnership with my students. This led me to do a master's thesis on LOGO at the University of New Mexico. By then I had the graduate school bug and wanted to go as far as I could with my education. This was when I discovered the field of LDT, though at that time it went by many different names, such as *instructional systems*, the name of the Ph.D. program at Penn State I eventually completed. I have yet to meet someone who has a story quite like mine. And as you tell your story, I'll bet it is just as unique.

The stories I've heard from graduate students over my 35 years as a professor of LDT about how it is that they now find themselves sitting in my class continue to amaze and delight me. I have come to appreciate what this has meant for our field. I think these seemingly haphazard journeys of people finding their way to the LDT field has resulted in an incredibly eclectic and diverse bunch of people with skills and experiences that seem to run the full range of work experiences. Our field seems to have become a kind of safe haven or refuge for creative people who started out in jobs that often did not take full advantage of their creativity. I have worked with countless students who were working in jobs with good careers in front of them, but for

Foreword **xiii**

whatever reason they found themselves becoming bored or disillusioned with their actual day-to-day job duties. Almost all had become highly skilled in some area but began yearning for something that would tap into their creative spirits while being challenged to work and help others. The LDT field offered them a chance for more fulfilling work.

As I welcome new students to the LDT field, I often will show a clip from the movie *Dead Poets Society* of the moment when English teacher John Keating, played by Robin Williams, tries to explain to his very privileged white male students why they should read and write poetry:

> We don't read and write poetry because it's cute. We read and write poetry because we are members of the human race. And the human race is filled with passion. And medicine, law, business, engineering, these are noble pursuits and necessary to sustain life. But poetry, beauty, romance, love, these are what we stay alive for. To quote from Whitman, "O me! O life! . . . of the questions of these recurring; of the endless trains of the faithless . . . of cities filled with the foolish; what good amid these, O me, O life?" Answer. That you are here – that life exists, and identity; that the powerful play goes on and you may contribute a verse. *That the powerful play goes on and you may contribute a verse. What will your verse be?*

I want my new students to know that the LDT field offers many exciting possibilities for the verse they will contribute, even though they don't know yet what that verse will be. But I think this little movie clip tells us even more. I've always thought that *learning* should have been included in Mr. Keaton's list of the things we in the human race stay alive for. The ultimate mission for those of us in the LDT field is to help people learn and perform to the best of their talents and abilities. And what could be more noble than that?

The chapters in this book offer you some examples of how creative individuals have harnessed past careers and experiences to move the LDT field forward. As you read, take some notes about how you think your work experiences up to this point might serve you well as you turn this exciting corner in your career path. Those notes will come in handy when it is your turn to write the follow-up chapters.

Lloyd Rieber
Professor of Learning, Design, and Technology
University of Georgia

Preface

The Multi-disciplinary Instructional Designer aims to capture a critical conversation among practitioners, which has yet to be addressed from a literary perspective. Instructional design itself is a well-established and documented field and is often linked with other specializations such as cognitive learning theory, education, project management, graphic design, and programming. Yet many professionals who choose to become instructional designers have backgrounds which reflect far greater intellectual diversity. Ask any instructional designer you meet what their background is, and you will receive answers such as music, clergy, mathematics, social work, architecture, and many more. Each of these professions are well established and have their own manifesto of accompanying skills and knowledge which have been cultivated over years and in some cases centuries.

Even though instructional design is deeply rooted in research, it is still a relatively young profession. In fact, we can draw similarities between the instructional design profession and a developing artist. The first portion of an artist's journey is dedicated to learning the technical skill required to create a work of art. In the age of artisans, a young apprentice would learn these skills by copying the work of the most accomplished experts. Once an apprentice was able to create a flawless duplicate of the original work, they were then given the creative freedom to craft their own works based on things that inspired them. This is what much of the literature on instructional design has done. By drawing on the influences of learning theories, the profession of instructional design has been established. Unfortunately, the instructional design field has yet to venture away from the work of the traditional visionaries to create a literary piece that captures the inspiration that resides in the world around us. That is the purpose of this book: to seek inspiration from professions other than our own and blend them with the work that designers passionately pursue on a daily basis.

Throughout this book, the reader will notice that we use multiple terms to describe the working contexts of an instructional designer. While developing this text, we wanted to capture the varied experiences of the contributing authors. As such, we feel it important to explain the differences in terminology:

1. Consultant/designer/learning designer/learning scientist are all terms that can be used to describe the titular instructional designer. As evidenced by the experiences in the author's chapters, this is a type of role that can range significantly but at the core is someone with expertise to create positive learning experiences.
2. Subject matter expert (SME)/client/faculty are all terms that can be used to describe individuals or groups partnering with the instructional designer and bringing their expertise to help inform the topic of a training or other education experience being developed.
3. Learner and student are also used to represent both the informal and formal venues for learning.

As you read across this text, we hope that this brief explanation of terms helps you navigate from chapter to chapter.

A Closer Look at Instructional Design

1

*Carl S. Moore, Ph.D.
and Julaine Fowlin, Ph.D.*

Introduction

Imagine the following scenarios. A subject matter expert (SME) came to an ID consultation for a course they were asked to develop and teach for the first time. They are excited but overwhelmed and question if they are the right person for the course they are teaching. During the consultation session the instructional designer reflects back to the SME what they hear the specific needs are and is able to isolate the information for the course mode, outcomes, activities, assessments, and other situational factors. The instructional designer was also able to provide a larger context as to how the course connects and sequences with the curriculum of the academic program and most importantly the value that the SME brings to the learning context. After much trepidation, the SME leaves the session feeling more confident in their ability to teach the course and with a clearer mind. While they are in the session, they also talk about the SME's upcoming faculty portfolio narrative and how to make sure their teaching, service, and scholarship activities are best evidenced and communicated in their narrative. When the SME leaves, they remark, "Thank you so much, I had no idea you could help me with all that. Glad I came. You are definitely more than an instructional designer."

DOI: 10.4324/9781003268413-1

In another scenario, an institutional leader who has an ID background is participating on an ad hoc institution-wide strategic planning committee. After a few long meetings of deliberation, this individual suggests that the group consider mapping their ideas to the charge that was provided by the provost. To simplify this, the person uses a three-column table displaying the overarching goals that everyone has agreed-upon, some potential activities in the next column, and actions that seem to be working towards those overarching goals in the last column. People on the committee are thankful for the clarity that is provided, and some are actually surprised at how helpful the visualization of the process was for them. One of the committee members asks, "Wow, do you do strategic planning often, or were you on the strategic planning committee before?" The person responds, "No, but I do have an instructional design background, and what we do at the course level is what we're doing at the institutional level right now. Same skills."

These two scenarios are just a glimpse of the diversity of tasks that instructional designers perform, but they both reflect a shared feeling in organizations regarding the power of instructional design to achieve outcomes in a way that is both people- and task-centric.

The label of ID is growing in popularity, especially since many more education and business entities need to draw on the skill set to create agile learning experiences. However, the true understanding of the range of an IDs ability is still limited and needs to be teased out even for those who are familiar and can see the value of the ID services.

The value of instructional design (ID) is often misunderstood not because of its lack of importance nor is it unclear because of its lack of articulated essential skills. The issue is that the range of work performed by ID professionals is so dynamic and shows up differently depending on the setting, passion, interest, prior background, etc. (Larson & Lockee, 2004; Richey et al., 2011). Often those who are unfamiliar (and many are) with the core skill set of instructional designers (IDs) put us in a defined box. This mindset creates challenges and can result in organizations not leveraging the full potential that IDs can contribute to achieving organizational outcomes. For example, when we are viewed only as instructional specialists, organizations will miss opportunities to receive assistance, leadership, and/or collaboration in other areas that are within any given instructional designer's ability. Some of this misunderstanding is due to a limited understanding of learning what it is, when and how it can occur, and our roles both in formal and informal learning. Unless one has studied learning sciences, they might not understand that learning is broad and occurs at micro, meso, and macro levels. Learning can occur in a formal classroom but can also occur in non-structured ways. In fact in many organizations there has been increased emphasis on learning and development as intellectual capital is seen as a competitive advantage, thus an increase in emphasis on areas like knowledge management and performance improvement (Larson & Lockee, 2004). The instructional designer's role is a special one in that the component skills needed to perform this role are the heart of the skills needed to build, design, and implement learning and performance solutions in any type of setting. As Stefaniak (2020) points out, "While . . . instructional design may comprise one unit or area within an organization, the long-term implications are widespread. Training has the potential to affect knowledge management, succession planning, customer relations, and strategic business operations" (p. 1).

What Is Instructional Design? Who Are Instructional Designers?

It is probably a running joke among instructional designers that we all have this deeply tacit, embedded, and shared understanding among each other about what we do, what Wagner (2011) calls the "secret handshake," but we struggle to fully articulate to others what we do and oftentimes when we try, we are still met with blank stares and a series of clarifying questions. This is largely due to the fact that the field of instructional design is ever-changing (Larson & Lockee, 2004). Interestingly, over 30 years ago (Schiffman, 1986, p. 14) stated, "Ambiguity seems to shroud the field of instructional systems design (ISD)" and to date, it seems that this may still be the case. However, despite changes and diversity in practice, we believe there are some basic tenets that can be used to establish a shared definition of the field. Notably, while we have used the term *instructional design* throughout this chapter, we must acknowledge that our field in some cases may be referred to as instructional systems design or instructional design and technology (IDT). Some definitions of instructional design refer to the field as focusing solely on instructional/training solutions, while other definitions reflect a shift to a more holistic view of performance problems (Rothwell et al., 2007). Richey et al., (2011) noted that most definitions tend to emphasize instructional design as a process; others include the scientific foundations and the products that may derive from a project, while others still focus on the function of instructional design in creating effective instruction.

Consider the Following Definitions

> Rothwell and Kazanas (2008): Instructional design means more than literally creating instruction. It is associated with the broader concept of analyzing human performance problems systematically, identifying the root causes of those problems, considering various solutions to address the root causes, and implementing the solutions in ways designed to minimize the unintended consequences of corrective action.
>
> (p. 3)

> Reiser (2001): The field of instructional design and technology encompasses the analysis of learning and performance problems, and the design, development, implementation, evaluation, and management of instructional and non-instructional processes and resources intended to improve learning and performance in a variety of settings, particularly educational institutions and the workplace. Professionals in the field of instructional design and technology often use systematic instructional design procedures and employ a variety of instructional media to accomplish their goals.
>
> (p. 1)

> Branch (2009, p. 9): "Instructional design centers on individual learning, has immediate and long-range phases, is systematic, and uses a systems approach about knowledge and human learning. . . . Instructional design is an iterative process of planning performance objectives, selecting instructional strategies, choosing media and selecting or creating materials, and evaluation."

There are times when we are called into situations where instruction is not the solution; therefore we are trained to do a thorough analysis to make that determination. Some of us possess additional knowledge and skill sets to be able to contribute to non-instructional solutions. It is here that the line may be blurred with a sister field known as human performance technology, which is defined by the International Society for Performance Improvement (ISPS) on their website as "a systematic approach to improving productivity and competence, uses a set of methods and procedures – and strategy for solving problems – for realizing opportunities related to the performance of people." This additional skill set is acknowledged by the International Board of Standards for Training, Performance, and Instruction (ibstpi) as an advanced instructional design competency.

As you will see in this multi-disciplinary book, we show up in different and expansive ways, and thus we embrace a holistic approach akin to Richey et al.'s (2011) definition: "ID is the science and art of creating detailed specifications for the development, evaluation, and maintenance of situations which facilitate learning and performance." (p. 3) **Simply put, we would say instructional designers are in the business of strategic learning and performance improvement.**

"The field of instructional design integrates knowledge from many fields such as psychology, education, communications, management, systems theory, and social science" (Schiffman, 1986, p. 14). Thus, as we seek to articulate our identity, it may help to go beyond a definition to examining what Richey et al., (2011) call the instructional design knowledge base. They represent the ID knowledge base as an intersection of six domains that they believe address the most pertinent ID concepts, processes, and research. As you explore the subsequent chapters, this framework will be helpful.

1. Learners and Learning Processes
2. Learning and Performance Contexts
3. Content Structure and Sequence
4. Instructional and Non-instructional Strategies
5. Media and Delivery Systems
6. Designers and Design Processes

When was the field of instructional design born? While a detailed history of the field of instructional design is outside of the scope of this chapter, a synopsis may help us to understand the origins of the nature of the field. We also acknowledge that instructional design is worldwide, but for this segment, we will focus on the historical context in the US. Instructional design as a discipline has evolved over 70 years. Reiser (2001) provides a detailed historical account, noting that the development of training programs during World War II was a pivotal time in the history of instructional design in the United States. During this time, the military called on psychologists and educators to conduct research and develop training. Among the influential people were Robert Gagné, Leslie Briggs, and John Flanagan, who based their work on "instructional principles derived from research and theory on instruction, learning, and human behavior" (p. 2). After World War II many of the people involved continued the work and the perspective of training as a system emerged, leading to B.F. Skinner's programmed instruction movement in the mid 1950s and 1960s. Programmed instruction was based on a

6 Carl S. Moore and Julaine Fowlin

systematic controlled approach of breaking down and sequencing instruction for individual learning using operant conditioning (use of rewards and stimulus-response to govern behavior). During this time there was also a renewed emphasis on learner objectives by Robert Mager and then Benjamin Bloom. We say renewed as Ralph Tyler is considered the father of objectives from the 1930s. Then in the 1960s, Robert Glasser started the criterion-referenced testing movement, where learners' performance was assessed against competencies instead of compared to a group. By 1965 Robert Gagné published the *Conditions of Learning* focused on five domains of learning:

1. Verbal Information
2. Intellectual Skills
3. Psychomotor Skills
4. Attitudes
5. Cognitive Strategies

Gagné posited that each domain requires a different set of conditions, and he also developed the famous nine events of instruction. Gagné's movement also brought about a move from more behaviorist approaches to more cognitive information processing approaches, which gave rise to techniques like a learner and task analysis. Jumping ahead, in the 1970s many instructional design models were developed, and instructional design processes flourished in many settings, such as academia, military, and industry. This also resulted in many graduate programs being created. In the 1980s there was significant interest in using microcomputers for instructional purposes, and it was also around this time that the HPT movement gained traction with a focus on performance and non-instructional solutions to performance problems. By the 20th century, constructivism and other similar perspectives became popular as well as distance education. This was also the era where the expansion of our work to areas such as knowledge management, where instructional designers work with organizations to strategically convert individual tacit knowledge to organizational knowledge, led to organizations focusing less on formal training programs to designing knowledge management systems. Please see eLearning Infographics [https://elearninginfographics.com/brief-history-instructional-design-infographic/] and Instructional Design Central [www.instructionaldesigncentral.com/instructional-design-history] for graphical illustrations of the history of the field.

This historical account captures a few of the key moments. While the exact dates and facts are important, we think it is even more essential to leave with the overarching understanding that the history of the field represents openness to changes in society, discoveries of research, and a wider view of what learning is in multiple places. This may explain why some people have advocated that we be called **learning scientists** and not instructional designers even though within the profession we know that the term "instruction" is used broadly to the outsider; it has a limited view to formal training. Whether we will have uniformed names is still yet to be determined, but we could probably start with a shared repertoire about what unifies us in this multi-disciplinary space. What unifies us is an emphasis on contextual designs and understanding that no two designs are the same even in the same organization. As Cennamo and Kalk (2019) highlight, instructional design is not a cookbook approach; our work is beautifully messy and iterative. They highlight three components of design that we believe are core tenets of what we do and allow us to embrace the multi-disciplinary goodness of this book.

1. Design involves conversations around critical issues.
2. Design is an iterative knowledge-building cycle.
3. Design is a collaborative activity among individuals representing different perspectives and expertise.

As we wrap up this section regarding our core identity, there is a need to pause and reflect on how each of us as professionals can exercise our agency in compassionately dispelling some of the myths around the field. Additionally, there is a call to action for instructional design programs to ensure there is alignment between the competencies in the formal curriculum with professional standards and the demands of society (Guerra-López & Joshi, 2021). Furthermore, as this book highlights, instructional designers come from a wide array of backgrounds, thus instructional design programs also need to consider how to make room for unique professional identity formation that comes from the blend and integration of multiple disciplines.

Dispelling the Misconceptions

As we seek to define the field and who we are as professionals, it is worth taking some time to articulate who we are not. We know examples and non-examples can help learners to fully understand certain concepts. We believe the same may apply to helping others understand our field. Schiffman (1986) encapsulates the views which often govern the misconception of our field. We believe **the most dominant one is what they call the media view**, where others believe instructional design is all about the

8 Carl S. Moore and Julaine Fowlin

selection of hardware and software. While we are sometimes involved in these conversations, it is usually done in collaboration with an instructional technologist or computer scientist. Next is the embryonic systems view, where some believe we are all about media production, such as storyboards, video recording, editing, and so forth. While we use media affordances to optimize learning, our goal is not media production; this role is often termed instructional media specialist or digital media specialist. Following is the narrow systems view where our work is viewed as linear, step-by-step, and prescriptive. This view is often evidenced in consultations where an SME may be looking for precise solutions when the famous instructional design response is usually "it depends" as we consider so many variables in decision-making, and as mentioned before our work is iterative. Next is the standard systems thinking view, where it is believed we adopt a strictly behavioral approach to learning and instruction. As seen in the history and definition **we operate from a systems** thinking mindset, where we take time to determine when training is an appropriate solution versus when it is not. Schiffman (1986) reinforces that "ISD is more than a simple method. **It is a field requiring a wide range of psychological, sociological, interpersonal, and managerial skills if it is to be skillfully and creatively practiced" (p. 20).**

In examining these views and titles that do not define us, our attention is drawn not only to our identity as professionals but what we would like to call the **"instructional design mindset." The instructional designer is a capacity based systems thinker who is emotionally intelligent and maintains a growth mindset.** In the chapter Out of the Frying Pan – Into the Fire: The Unintended (and Amazing) Consequences of Risk-Taking and the Practice of Instructional Design, Desmarais articulates it well when he states that

> To be an optimist is to embrace hope above all things. . . . To be an instructional designer requires the same growth mindset, the same belief that it will be better next time, and the same belief in the power of persistence and iterative development as Churchill articulated so profoundly in his nation's darkest hour.

We therefore adopt what Schiffman (1986, p. 16) calls the instructional systems design view, which is a

> synthesis of theory and research related to (a) how humans perceive and give meaning to the stimuli in their environments, (b) the nature of information and how it is composed and transmitted, (c) the concept of

systems and the interrelationships among factors promoting or deterring efficient and effective accomplishment of the desired outcomes (Torkelson, 1977), and (d) the consulting and managerial skills necessary to meld points a through c into a coherent whole.

As Jill E. Stefaniak highlights in "Lessons From the Barre: The Intersection Between Dance and Dynamical Design Decision-Making" systems thinking is crucial to the work we do as "Our abilities to design solutions are inherently dependent on our ability to interact with and evolve with the people, processes, and objects that comprise our systems." With this in mind we will transition to exploring some of the skill sets that an instructional designer brings to the table and how our mindset and way of thinking allows us to contribute to organizational outcomes in ways that organizations may not realize we have the capacity to.

Instructional Designer Skills

At the very beginning of this chapter, we started off discussing two different scenarios that put the instructional designer skills on display. One was related to a traditional view of an instructional designer helping to build a course. But if you might recall, the same course design skills were also the ones that could help a faculty member see how to align the artifacts for their dossier. While those same skills did that for the dossier, they were also helpful in a strategic planning situation, where everyone needed to be able to map goals to institution activities and establish accountability measures for those goals. One might ask themselves, what do you call these skills? Well, it's the presence of a wide range of competencies we highlighted and will continue to unpack in this section. But first, we would like you **to try this.** Below, you will see what many instructional designers referred to as a three-column alignment table. Think about one activity that you have to do that is not teaching and learning related. Let's say it's even a goal that you may have established recently.

In the first column (far left) of Table 1.1, list your goal. In the middle column list as many things as you can that would help you achieve that goal, and in the last column articulate how you will know you achieved your goal. As you can see in the example below, the person has a goal that they will eat healthy meals three times a day. The actions that they will take to do the goal are listed to advance that goal, and the accountability measures are ways the person will be able to measure their progress.

10 Carl S. Moore and Julaine Fowlin

Table 1.1 Three-column table

Goal	Actions/Activities	Accountability Measure/Assessments
Eat a healthy meal three times a day	- Read about nutrition - Take cooking classes - Watch YouTube videos - Google healthy restaurants near job	- Track meals in an app - Discuss meal choices with partner daily
What is your goal?	**What activities and actions will you perform to achieve this goal?**	**How will you measure your progress and hold yourself accountable?**

After you complete the aforementioned, you will have participated in an activity instructional designers might engage in to establish alignment. In many instructional design instances, the goal is something related to learning, the activities are learning activities, and the assessments are exams, tests, quizzes, assignments, and so forth. One of the powerhouse skills of an instructional designer is making sure the stated goals of the endeavor correlates with whatever activities or actions are going to take place and that there is a way in which an individual, unit, and/or organization can clearly know whether those stated goals have been met. We can look at an instructional designer as a GPS for any project or organization. If you provide the instructional designer with the destination that you would like to get to, their skills allow them to calculate the route to get there. Similar to a GPS, IDs can process the information you give them and fill in the steps on how to get you and others to the stated goals and milestones along your path.

There are a host of competencies that IDs maintain that are best understood when they manifest themselves in any specific functional area. For example, Carl has a background in television production. When we are creating treatments for any program or plotting out the scope and sequence for a show, we use the same approach for alignment to make sure the times match up with the activities that we are doing for that specific time and that everything fits together. So in some ways we could say that Carl's background in television production informed his ability to be an instructional designer and vice versa, and that's the beauty of it. You will be reading in the chapters that follow a wide range of ways in which ID skills show up in different functional areas. However, here we would like to focus on two broader constructs that apply to every organization: project management and change management.

Project Management

Gido and Clements (2014, p. 4) refer to a project as "an endeavor to accomplish a specific objective through a unique set of interrelated tasks and the effective utilization of resources." IDs are masters at the aforementioned. According to amp.org, project management is "the application of processes, methods, skills, knowledge and experience to achieve specific project objectives according to the project acceptance criteria within agreed parameters." The site also notes that "project management has final deliverables that are constrained to a finite timescale and budget." Though, we don't doubt that instructional designers can impact final deliverables connected to time and budget, we are going to stick with the first part of this definition to explicate the project management skills of IDs.

When many people consider the role of an instructional designer, they may think about the actual task of walking a person through building a course. We hope after reading this chapter that you see this as a limited view. Vieger (2020) referred to ID as a concierge that "act[s] as a project manager in charge of keeping all assigned course projects on track" (p. 26). The full scope of the arsenal of instructional designer abilities show up most prominently when it comes to building curriculum and courses. When building a singular course or curriculum, IDs are working on the initiative as a project (Pan, 2012). This project has its own objectives, agreed-upon parameters, and timeline, all of which have to be managed by the ID. So when designing a course, an ID works as a project manager from the beginning of the project to its completion. The same is true in the reverse when looking at the operations of a project manager that might work in any industry. Let's say you have a project manager who is working for a Fortune 500 company. They have specific goals, targets, and activities that they need to track and report on; they are using instructional design skills to do this.

Serving as a project manager is one of the very prominent and important skills of IDs; another is the consultation aspect. A project manager at a fortune 500 company has to assemble groups, meet with key stakeholders, and work as a consultant to them. An instructional designer in a traditional college setting might have a consultation one-on-one with a subject matter expert (SME) or a dean. But both have to be able to reflect, perspective take, listen, summarize, synthesize, analyze, and communicate with the SME they are working with in a way that will assure the best possible outcome (Margerison, 2001). In consultation, it is important that the instructional designer is highly skilled at being able to hold a mirror up to the person(s) they are working with in order for them to clearly see what they are articulating and only then will the instructional designer be able to best help in achieving the desired outcome. Some may view consultation as an opportunity to provide advice. However, any such view of consultation is misinformed because the highly skilled instructional designer who is providing consultation is there to be curious in their aims to meet the needs of the stakeholders the best way they can. After it is clearly understood what the person and or group would like to do, the instructional designer then can suggest technology, strategies, and approaches that can best meet needs while producing the best possible product within the given constraints. But, as you can see, any suggestions cannot be made effectively without sound consultation and project management skills.

Change Management

Change management is another important competency that an instructional designer maintains (Schroeder, 2012; Vieger, 2020). We discussed the wide range of skills and abilities that instructional designers possess and helped you understand how these skills show up in areas that aren't dealing with the classroom. You will hear more about many transferable skills and examples throughout this book. For example, in Dudek's *Feminist Approaches to Instructional Design,* she notes that

> Instructional designers often hold essential roles as change agents within organizations because we facilitate how [power-based] questions get asked and how they are answered . . . we deal with fundamentally political and power-based questions; "what should be learned" and "how should it be organized.

However, if you were to isolate one of the central purposes of the instructional design position, it would be to improve learning performance. By virtue of the role being there to have a continuous improvement approach, there is an underlying constructivist ideology informing the work of instructional designers – one that automatically invites ideas, explores, and wants to propose solutions and actions that best meet the needs of learners/the organization. All of this adds up to change management that happens in the classroom or boardroom, impacts the academic program or initiative, and ultimately can have an impact on the institution and or organization overall (Paton & McCalman, 2008). So at their core, by virtue of performing their job, instructional designers are change agents. Change agents who have change management skills as a core competency.

Another thing to consider is that learning itself is a change of behavior. So, in traditional education settings, instructional designers are particularly impactful in promoting that learning occurs in a classroom to a greater degree, while at the same time helping SME construct learning experiences. In settings where the person is designing a training program for athletes or any other field, they are also still encouraging a change of behavior. We are designed to think about systems and the changes that can be promoted on micro, meso, and macro levels (Stefaniak, 2020; Schroeder, 2012).

You'll see more details about how the instructional design field itself can help us view change management in the instructional design process in other chapters of this book as well as other ways the skills instructional designers possess help organizations evolve.

Conclusion

The value of an instructional designer and/or their skill set is often not fully realized. We hope that throughout this book you are able to understand the intricacies of the ID field and individuals that perform the role in a way that allows for you to imagine, beyond the examples provided, how such individuals could contribute to any given endeavor. We venture to say that as long **as something needs to be done and or learned, the instructional designer skill set is of value**.

While we aim to provide clarity regarding the boundaries of the field, our hope is that individuals and institutions will have an understanding of the basic tenets of the field and the professionals accompanied by an openness and appreciation for the diversity of positionality and skill sets that an instructional designer may bring to the table. We encourage organizations to treat each instructional designer as an embodiment of their training, the setting in which they operate, their passion and interest, and prior background. A food analogy may serve us well in this case, viewing the tenets of instructional design as the general recipe for a cookie dough but allowing room for the diversity of textures and flavors to come out in the sweetness of the final product after its baked.

Reference List

Branch, R.M. (2009). *Instructional design: The ADDIE approach* (Vol. 722). Springer Science & Business Media.

Cennamo, K., & Kalk, D. (2019). *Real world instructional design: An iterative approach to designing learning experiences*. Routledge.

Gido, J., & Clements, J. (2014). *Successful project management*. Cengage Learning.

Guerra-López, I., & Joshi, R. (2021). A study of instructional design master's programs and their responsiveness to evolving professional expectations and employer demand. *The Journal of Applied Instructional Design, 10*(2). KalkCennamoP210_instructionaldesign intherealworld.

Larson, M.B., & Lockee, B.B. (2004). Instructional design practice: Career environments, job roles, and a climate of change. *Performance Improvement Quarterly, 17*(1), 22–40.

Margerison, C.J. (2001). *Managerial consulting skills: A practical guide*. Gower Publishing, Ltd.

Pan, C.C. (2012). A symbiosis between instructional systems design and project management. *Canadian Journal of Learning and Technology/La revue canadienne de l'apprentissage et de la technologie, 38*(1), 4–9.

Paton, R.A., & McCalman, J. (2008). *Change management: A guide to effective implementation*. Sage.

Reiser, R.A. (2001). A history of instructional design and technology: Part II: A history of instructional design. *Educational Technology Research and Development, 49*(2), 57–67.

Richey, R.C., Klein, J.D., & Tracey, M.W. (2011). *The instructional design knowledge base: Theory, research, and practice*. Routledge.

Rothwell, W.J., Hohne, C.K., & King, S.B. (2007). *Human performance improvement: Building practitioner competence*. Elsevier/Butterworth-Heinemann.

Rothwell, W.J., & Kazanas, H. (2008). *Mastering the instructional design process: A systematic approach*. Pfeiffer.

Schiffman, S.S. (1986). Instructional systems design: Five views of the field. *Journal of Instructional Development, 9*(4), 14–21.

Schroeder, C. (2012). *Coming in from the margins: Faculty development's emerging organizational development role in institutional change*. Stylus Publishing, LLC.

Stefaniak, J. (2020). The utility of design thinking to promote systemic instructional design practices in the workplace. *TechTrends, 64*(2), 202–210.

Torkelson, G. (1977). AVCR–One quarter of a century: Evolution of theory and research. *AVCR, 25*(4), 317–358.

Vieger, R. (2020). A concierge model. In F. Darby (Ed.), *The learner-centered instructional designer: Purposes, processes, and practicalities of creating online courses in higher education* (pp. 223–226). Stylus Publishing, LLC.

Wagner, E. (2011). Essay: In search of the secret handshakes of ID. *The Journal of Applied Instructional Design, 1*(1), 33–37. https://edtechbooks.org/-JJy

A Consultative Mindset **2**

Aligning Strategic Learning Initiatives Using Marketing-Based Approaches

Robyn A. Defelice, Ph.D.

Robyn's Story

As an instructional designer (ID), how would you go about treating the topic of hybrid corn? This one question alone has already begun spinning my ID mental wheels. The questions being conjured range from wondering about the audience to what content the training will cover (and probably, "Why hybrid corn?"). There are obviously many more queries in between, focusing on delivery and implementation and level and depth of learner interactions, and so on.

This discussion on corn in my media theory course, while gaining my terminal degree, was a pivotal moment in seeing the intersection of two of my careers: marketing and instructional design. After nearly 9 years of practicing in the field as a learning and development consultant to a stratification of industries, my mind just naturally thinks in these multifaceted ways. At this moment, though, I was realizing I had not been considering my aptitude for marketing and how it's played a part in assisting my clients.

For example, if I had posed the same question to a marketing director, unequivocally, I would ask parallel questions to those that I would as an

DOI: 10.4324/9781003268413-2

ID. Though some may disagree, the marketing professional would also be attempting to find the need surrounding hybrid corn to create a solution, whether that was how to get more people to eat hybrid corn or influence farmers' use of hybrid corn seed by discussing the environmental benefits and so on.

At that moment, I realized that marketing goals are not any different than those of an ID. Marketing is the process of offering informational or persuasive solutions to a problem for the purposes of awareness and/or action. Likewise, instructional design is the process of offering training solutions to a problem associated with a group or individual. The marketing professional must take into consideration similar factors as the instructional designer. However, a key difference is that marketing focuses on return on investment or ROI (whether money, behavior modification, etc.). For example, in managing the marketing for a magisterial candidate, my goal was to influence people to vote for this individual. The ROI was the candidate winning (hopefully).

While some IDs will claim that training can demonstrate ROI, it often does not, as learning products rarely align to a business driver, which are things that have a major impact on the performance of the business itself. For example, sales or product quality. However, training materials are often stored in a system that can tell you usage, completion, and passing rates. That's part of what is often used to calculate ROI in training, but it is not enough information to prove that the newly acquired knowledge or skills had an impact on performance. These data points do not tell us if the training contributed to better sales or ensuring a quality product. Exercising a consultative marketing mentality is an opportunity for the ID, and its L&D department, to demonstrably contribute to the overall success of the organization.

The common challenge that takes away this critical aspect for IDs is being rushed to just produce training for a perceived problem, not an actual problem. Analysis is often cursory and more so based on the premise of taking orders rather than being consultative, which a marketing associate is to their client (Michaels, 2018). In fact, research performed by ATD (Association for Talent Development) denotes managers in corporate settings find that only 38% of training developed meets the needs of its intended audience (ATD Research, 2015).

If a marketing agency offered that as a success rate for their clients, that marketing agency wouldn't continue to exist! Marketing strategies are developed using a methodical approach that ascertains information every step of the way to ensure that the time and effort invested into the solution achieves that specified business goal. This cannot be said of ID practices, as ID practices often feel restrained by organization and client demands.

Overlaying the ID process with marketing approaches can help project stakeholders invest in the effort as a business decision, not as independent to business functions. For example, when a marketing project starts, it focuses on comprehending the business need, whereas instructional design focuses on the learning need. This chapter shares insights on pairing marketing and consultative principles to a traditional instructional design process, specifically surrounding solution creation and evaluation. These points are salient to any instructional designer in any industry, whether higher education, non-profit, corporate, government, and so forth.

Solving Problems and Creating Solutions

Client management and solution creation can be viewed through the lens of a marketing initiative. This is done because traditional ID practices for a needs analysis do not typically yield a partnership with the client. It is often an interview to gather project requirements, risks, and constraints. Or in other words, "just take the training order and make it."

As you can imagine this doesn't feel very consultant-like at all, let alone what an ID consultant wants for their client. To guide and advise on a solution, a consultant needs to be able to build trust and rapport with their client. They do this through asking questions that help them better understand a client's problem. A consultant then shares knowledge and expertise to create a solution.

One challenge with instructional design is that clients are not usually versed in instructional design theory or practices. Whereas in marketing, the client usually knows quite a bit about their product or program. The client can easily comprehend the concept of marketing as a method to attract and gain consumers. Many IDs work with clients that see their learners as an already previously acquired audience that is captive or must learn.

Therefore, the client does not think they need to attract or gain their learning audience. Not to mention that the jargon of ID is not necessarily intuitive or palatable to a client. The process of creating training is often distilled down to make it look nice or ensure there is a lot of engagement as requested by the client. In the client's mind that is all that is needed to make sure the captive audience learns.

The client would never request this of a marketing consultant mainly because the client is turning to the marketing consultant as an investment towards future gains. Those gains could be more consumers, more advocates, more adherences, and so on. The client doesn't often see the need for training in the same manner.

If an ID treats solution creation through the lens of a marketing problem, they may have more success in impacting business success (to a degree, organization culture around learning and development is a factor that is not addressed in this chapter but a variable worthy of being noted).

In reflecting on marketing's influence as part of the hybrid corn seed quandary, I thought about my time working for a local office product store in the late 1990s. I'll call them Office Place. They were not sure how to increase sales through a new marketing channel called e-commerce. I leaned into my skills for research and analysis, a cornerstone in my undergraduate studies, to determine the problems e-commerce would solve and the target market that had those problems.

Three years later, with my instructional design master's degree in hand, I was working with a manufacturing plant. I will just call them We Make Things, Inc. and they wanted equipment and team-building training. We Make Things, Inc. claimed that the new equipment was creating team-based issues, and productivity overall was on the decline. In their mind the only thing that could fix this issue was training.

In the first scenario, my client saw opportunity, but couldn't define it. In my second situation my client saw a problem and thought it was well defined. In both situations I needed to follow a process to identify or validate the opportunities and problems, discover critical factors that would shape a solution, develop an optimal solution, create products that supported that solution, and finally implement that solution and evaluate the efficacy of it.

For IDs that common process is ADDIE (analysis, design, development, implementation, evaluation), whereas marketers do not have a coined acronym but have a similar process for planning marketing strategies. Table 2.1 breaks down the two processes as aligned to ADDIE.

In comparison these processes look quite similar. Both occupations seek to determine if and what the problem is before moving into solution creation and so on. However, as described earlier in the chapter, it is common for *analysis* to be minimal or non-existent for the ID. It is more so a requirement-gathering phase, which doesn't lend itself at all to being consultative. The realization of these variances doesn't automatically turn into success for instructional designers. We have to find ways to incorporate these best practices from marketing into our L&D department's ID process.

A Consultative Mindset **19**

Table 2.1 A comparison of processes for finding and solving problems and providing solutions

Phases of a Problem	Common ID Process	Common Marketing Strategy Process
Problem-finding (Analysis)	Define the true nature of the problem through assessing the learner, the learning environment, and the content	Define the market segments (the audiences you intend on targeting) and comprehend the needs of that market
Problem-solving (Design)	Outline and structure a solution or solutions in preparation for development	Determine the solution or solutions that address the identified needs
Solution creation (Development)	Create the solution(s) using the format, modalities, and mediums selected	Create the solution(s) using various mediums to communicate with the target market
Solution delivery (Implementation)	Deliver the solution(s) via the selected method(s) to the target market	Distribute the solution(s) within the target market
Solution efficacy (Evaluation)	Assess the efficacy of the solution(s) against the desired learning outcome	Monitor the impact of the solution(s) on the target market's identified needs

This gives way to trying out some new approaches! Take your next project and treat the conversation with the client as one would for a marketing initiative as opposed to common ID-based analysis questions like in Table 2.2.

REFLECTION ACTIVITY

Translating Concepts

Looking at Table 2.2 the left two columns summarize a common approach to analysis by an ID. The right two columns address how marketing consultants address analysis. Review both sides and determine

20 Robyn A. Defelice

which method you use. If you fall predominantly in the left columns, consider using the right columns. If you fall somewhere in between, determine how you can reshape analysis with more of a marketing mindset. Lastly, if you fall completely to the right columns, you are doing awesome!

An example of customer care agents as the audience is used to provide context.

Table 2.2 Comparison of needs analysis approaches for instructional designers and marketers

Needs Analysis Factor	ID Needs Analysis – Common Line of Inquiry	Marketing Analysis Factor	Marketing Needs Analysis – Common Line of Inquiry
Problem Identification	• What is the problem? • *For example, what problem is the customer care agent facing and/or creating?*	**ROI**	• Can you quantify what success looks like for the employees that take this training? • *For example, what will happen if the customer care team doesn't receive this training?*
Learner Requirements	• Who is creating and/or impacted by the problem? • *For example, are all agents having the same problem?*	**Segmentation**	• Is the target audience homogeneous? Does everyone have the same prerequisite level of knowledge?

Needs Analysis Factor	ID Needs Analysis – Common Line of Inquiry	Marketing Analysis Factor	Marketing Needs Analysis – Common Line of Inquiry
			Are there any incentives or advantages to learning this information or skill? • *For example, will customer care agents, working less than a year in their role, need additional training compared to employees with more than a year of experience?*
Training Requirements	• Is the training mandatory? • *For example, do we need to train every customer care agent?*	**Reach**	• Where will this information get the most exposure to the targeted group(s)? What types of issues trigger the need for this information? What time(s) of day increase the need for this information?

(Continued)

22   Robyn A. Defelice

Table 2.2   (Continued)

Needs Analysis Factor	ID Needs Analysis – Common Line of Inquiry	Marketing Analysis Factor	Marketing Needs Analysis – Common Line of Inquiry
			• For example, are customer care agents on the phone when this happens? On average how many times a day does a customer care agent encounter this problem?

Of course, you should find your own way to ask questions around these parameters and see if you notice a difference in how your colleague or client describes their needs. The process may be unnatural to you and/or your stakeholder at first, and you could find yourself relying on old habits (aka the two left columns). That leads us into maturity of a department and an organization in being agile to change and the culture the organization embraces towards learning and development, both of which are beyond the scope of this chapter.

But what we can focus on from the suggested activity is practicing a marketing mindset. Marketing processes focus on being able to advise on the best options to gain the best results. The same can be said about the ID even though the ID does not often get to practice being consultative. Looking at what comprises a consultative mindset can assist in maximizing marketing approaches in an ID context.

Developing a Consultative Mindset

If we return to the initial subject of hybrid corn, we can look at the research on mass marketing efforts targeted at farmers to adopt hybrid corn seed and

A Consultative Mindset **23**

note that they were not necessarily successful on their own. Research (Lowery & DeFleur, 1995) proved that it was a combination of interpersonal communication with repeated exposure to mass communications that accelerated adoption. In other words, farmers had influence over their neighboring farmers. The information that was mass distributed had less influence than the neighbor. Furthermore, the neighbors who had experimented with the seed had greater influence.

In essence, these farmers were consulting or sharing their knowledge and expertise with their peers. From planting a few acres to test the product, they could speak from direct experience. In turn peers used this information to guide decisions on adopting the new seed for themselves. That decision was the problem that needed to be solved by that farmer. Should they adopt the new seed or should they not?

The basics of a consultative mindset are rooted in an individual's ability to share their knowledge and expertise. This means that the individual has a good grasp of their portfolio of work and capabilities. They can speak to and use previous experiences to guide and inform the client's decision-making. The ability to share is only outweighed by what you know. To really sharpen your consultative mindset, start by performing some analysis on yourself and your L&D team (or involve them, that would be even better!) to create a profile of the department for purposes of decision-making towards strategic efforts.

REFLECTION ACTIVITY

Strategic Profile Development

Developing a strategic profile of an L&D team or department activity is best done when the ID can contextualize it to their current employment situation. For many this context will be as part of an L&D department or team. This means part of your knowledge and expertise comes from the work and capabilities of the department itself.

As consultants assist clients in achieving their strategic vision(s), so must you (or your L&D team) be able to help your clients achieve theirs. The question examples aligned to the marketing consultant in Table 2.2 above demonstrates a grasp of how to get clients to define the profile of their strategy, not necessarily the vision. Vision may not become fully articulated until a solution is formed. Solutions are derived from evaluating the strategic profile against the project constraints.

This means consultants must also have a strategic profile that they weigh against project constraints. For you and your L&D team to begin developing your own strategic profile, try the following exercise.

What you will need:

- Using a spreadsheet software, a data entry tool, or even a survey tool is recommended. The important thing is you will need to analyze your results both quantitatively and qualitatively and select a platform that will aid in mitigating data entry errors and more efficient analysis.

How to execute:

To begin, group information under broad categories:

- Training Topic – For example, new hires, compliance, HR related (e.g., timesheets, vacation)
- Product Type – For example, instructor-led training, self-paced eLearning, infographic, podcast
- Delivery Mechanism or Technology – For example, virtual via an online tool, LMS, intranet
- Target Audiences – For example, all employees, new hires, senior leadership, dayshift

For each category review the listed items and answer the following:

- How does it support the organization's strategic vision?
- How proactive (or reactive) does it make us in managing towards the strategic vision?
- Where can it provide value within the organization to drive strategic success?

A Consultative Mindset **25**

- What creates risk in it being valued as a contributing factor to the strategic success of the whole organization?

Draft a document that presents the strategic profile of the L&D department. Presentation of information could be based on the categories or the questions. Round out the profile by aligning it to any known strategic goals of the department and/or the organization itself.

This type of activity can be repeated to keep the profile aligned to the most current strategic plan. The key is to focus on 1–3 points per item, and if necessary, prioritize the points.

The activity above is not always easy when you're not often able to address how your L&D team's contributions play a part in driving organizational success. To some degree it's foreign thinking. To help elaborate the activity, the following example from one of my client's strategic profiles is provided.

GOOD STUFF, INC. L&D STRATEGIC PROFILE

The example focuses on the target audience category. The item selected from the category is new hires.

- How does the L&D team support the organization's strategic vision?
  - Perform a biannual meeting with the HR Manager for planning purposes. Each meeting is an opportunity to review joint initiatives, prioritize them, and share any new business or information in support of collaborative efforts.
  - Working with HR, senior leadership, and middle management to develop a coaching and mentoring program in preparation for an internal promotion program. The initiative is an effort to manage the forecasted 30% turnover due to retirements in the next three years.
- How proactive (or reactive) does it make us in managing towards the strategic vision?
  - An analysis of the organization's current strategic plan to determine where the L&D department aligns and/or has the

opportunity to strengthen alignment. This information will function as a baseline and lens to examine current and future initiatives.

- Common skill sets and competencies of the job roles are not known by the L&D team. In addition, the criteria used to evaluate performance is different in every department. Having the job specific information would allow for mapping current content to specific competencies and evaluative measures to determine if current job roles have gaps in their training curricula. A second analysis of this information will focus on determining if the current materials support the employee in being a successful contributor to the strategic vision.

- Where can it provide value within the organization to drive strategic success?
  - The current coaching initiative has placed the L&D department in a positive light. For example:
    - Senior leadership have approached the L&D team for a separate meeting to explore additional initiatives.
    - HR has recognized that the L&D team has not been treated as a partner at the table on previous initiatives. They have requested at the next biannual meeting to workshop a partnership agreement to ensure success.

- What creates risk in it being valued as a contributing factor to the strategic success of the whole organization?
  - Lack of data on new hires, such as turnover rates or expectations of competency in performing job (e.g., can perform 75% of their workload independently within 90 days of employment). Having better insight into what challenges departments are facing in keeping new hires and what expectations they have to assist in setting more realistic targets.

WRITE UP

Good Stuff Inc.'s L&D team acknowledges lacking comprehension of how they currently contribute to driving the success of the organization. The team also recognizes the need to develop baseline understandings to begin being more strategically focused. These realizations

> came about due to HR's strategic initiative with new hires. The L&D team is beginning to see new relationships forming within the organization due to this initiative and want to make sure they can support these new partnerships.
>
> There is also an opportunity to deepen pre-established ones with HR. For example, the L&D team envisions an opportunity to drive strategic success in acclimating new hires to their job roles more efficiently and effectively. They recognize the value of competency mapping to create targeted training and skill development. They will work more closely with HR to gather relevant data to help in developing a more holistic picture of the needs of new hires.

Focusing on problem identification and solution creation through the lens of a marketing consultant is intended to strengthen the ability to drive a different type of success for all involved. That success focuses on something greater than what IDs are used to presenting as success. L&D departments commonly provide information to stakeholders that demonstrate usage, consumption, and pass/fail rates, whereas a marketing consultant would present success as some form of return on investment (ROI), such as increase in sales, reduction in safety infractions, or even conversion of undecided to decided. The data L&D presents could be made more robust and address the same types of things noted in the previous sentence. L&D just needs to focus more on learning analytics for evaluation, not just usage.

Which brings us back to our hybrid corn seed. Success of adoption was studied to determine what had created adoption of the seed by all farmers in two prosperous farm communities. These findings have been the foundation to many things, one of which is understanding how to assist agriculturally focused companies to market to farmers more effectively.

A marketing consultant can use this information with their knowledge and expertise to create solutions that help companies achieve business goals that align to marketing initiatives. With marketing it's an assumed part of the process to share the findings of how successful an initiative was. Would you consider a marketing agency successful if a promotional campaign they created only yielded 1% increase in sales over a year for their client in a global market with few competitors? Probably not.

This example can be written off as a failure, but either way the marketing consultant is focused on sharing not only the success of the initiative, but also the return on investment or ROI of the effort. Perhaps sales are not strong,

28 Robyn A. Defelice

but the marketing consultant also provided information that changes the understanding of the consumer profile and how to approach educating them to become active consumers. It may not have achieved the desired strategic vision, but it informs it more than previous knowledge did, which is equally valuable.

There are also other stories that L&D departments can talk about as related to how they support other departments and teams throughout an organization. These stories come from measuring success against the quantified and/or qualified goals a team, department, or organization shares with the ID during analysis.

Sharing Success and Failure

As noted above from previous research by ATD (Association for Talent Development), the majority of L&D teams do not align their work to organizational outcomes mainly due to time constraints for appropriate analysis and being pigeon-holed into order taking roles as opposed to being consultative. Without this alignment it is hard for the L&D team to consult against it.

What can success look like for an ID and the L&D department? An example would be being able to tell your manager that the work you performed in creating templates for common project pieces has shown a decrease in project delays at the quality assurance phase. Now place this same success story at the level of the L&D department. To the organization the L&D team is demonstrating support towards organizational success through being efficient and cost-effective.

We've come to conclude that both marketing and ID are focused on educating a consumer. Each provides a targeted message, and once the message is received, there is an expectation of an action. However, the action and outcome in ID is much different than in marketing. In majority marketing entities will report success of action in quantifiable and qualitative manners. The following table outlines how an ID and a marketer commonly address outcomes of their initiatives:

Could you or your L&D department answer these marketing outcome questions? One point you could make is on *completion rates* as they are akin to *reach*, or how many individuals in your target audience were exposed to your message. Where L&D teams often cannot get with their clients is reporting where the training impact is taking effect (segmentation or which individuals in the target audience) and for the investment in that training what is the ROI? This information takes time to gather and analyze and requires designing an

A Consultative Mindset 29

Table 2.3 Similarities between instructional design and marketing initiatives

Common Training Outcomes	Training Product Outcomes	Common Marketing Outcomes	Marketing Campaign Outcomes
Passing Rates of Learners	• How many learners passed the exam at the minimum required passing score or higher? • For instance, the organization-wide mandatory compliance training had an 82% passing rate. • Out of the remaining 18%, 7% require remediation to pass successfully and 11% are delinquent in taking the compliance assessment.	**ROI – What does the organization expect to gain from the effort? (e.g., increased sales, decrease in accidents, etc.)**	• For the percentage reached, how much additional revenue was generated? If not revenue, how many individuals changed a behavior or habit (e.g., stopped smoking, complied with safety policies, etc.)? How many were unaware vs aware or aware vs undecided?
Perceived Satisfaction of Product by Learner	• Was the training experience meaningful to the learner? Does the learner think they can use the information or skills taught?	**Segmentation – Given the target audience, are there characteristics that you may group them by? (e.g., age, own home or rent, etc.)**	• Out of the percentage reached, what messages appealed to which sub-market(s) inside the targeted group? Were any messages

(Continued)

30 Robyn A. Defelice

Table 2.3 (Continued)

Common Training Outcomes	Training Product Outcomes	Common Marketing Outcomes	Marketing Campaign Outcomes
	• For example, 43% of the participants scored the instructor as a 10 (10 being Strongly Agree) in being knowledgeable on the topic.		universal to all sub-populations within the target?
Completion Rate of a Training Product	• How many of the target population took the training, whether completed or not? • 78% of the target audience completed 100% of the training. • 7% of the target audience started the training but have not completed it. • 15% of the target audience has not attempted the training.	**Reach – How many individuals in the target audience were exposed to the message?**	• If the target population was a million, what percentage of that population was captured with the marketing campaign?

A Consultative Mindset **31**

evaluative plan that would provide these answers. Following the theme of too little time and order taking, an organization often falls to wanting data that more so checks the box of being done as opposed to knowing what the training actually did for the individual and for the organization.

Is it more meaningful for you and/or your L&D team to share with hiring managers that all new hires took the training and passed it successfully? Or is it more valuable to inform the various stakeholders that the new hire onboarding training consistently results in the following:

- Supervisors cutting downtime and loss of productivity when introducing new staff into the mix
- New hires identifying the experience as building confidence in their ability to perform their job role
- Human resources reduction in new hire turnover

If this is not something your L&D department is doing, it can be difficult to regear your mindset to thinking in evaluative manners that share the success (or failure) of a learning initiative.

REFLECTION ACTIVITY

Measures of Success

Table 2.4 highlights an opportunity to think alternately on what data actually tells about the impact of a project as aligned to strategic initiatives. These measures of success (and failure) are more easily developed when the strategic profile and vision is known.

This activity is an opportunity to dig into your strategic profile and create strategically aligned measures towards a current or future L&D project. This effort will guide the beginnings of developing an evaluation plan, a great first step in being able to share results like a marketing consultant might.

Review the guidance in the table below and determine if you want to try and answer these on your own or with your L&D team first. If you have an internal champion that sits outside of L&D, such as a stakeholder that works with you often, see if they would be willing to perform this activity with you.

32 Robyn A. Defelice

The chart below is intended to guide and help define ROI, key segments in your target audience, and the reach that training is anticipated to have within the target audience and its respective segments.

This activity is not meant to be an absolute. For example, in performing this activity, you may define all the segments you are aware of, but as you track consumption, you may find different or more relevant segments than were previously determined.

As a recommendation, start small and focus on just one or two goals associated with your ROI. This will keep segmentation and reach more manageable. It will also give you an opportunity to examine the how, when, and what of your organization's learning data and analytics processes.

Table 2.4 Identifying project outcomes

Updated Training Outcome Categories	Defining What will Evaluate the Outcome(s)
ROI	• If no criteria have been established as a return on investment with the project, work with stakeholders to establish a baseline that addresses at least one goal that the stakeholder has, whether aligned to a departmental strategic initiative or an organization-focused one. • If the organization does not have a defined strategic plan, nor do the stakeholders, work with the stakeholders to establish a baseline and one measurable goal that demonstrates impact on the business (aka business driver).
Segmentation	• Determine if there are distinctions within the learning audience that may create variance to success. This could be related to seniority, time in job role, prerequisite knowledge, and so on.
Reach	Reach and gathering insight on it will be dependent on whether or not the subject matter has previously created training and if the target audience and

A Consultative Mindset **33**

Updated Training Outcome Categories	Defining What will Evaluate the Outcome(s)
	any or all segments have been provided that training – whether voluntarily consumed or required as part of the job. Otherwise, use these prompts to think about ensuring that you reach your total audience or what measures will be seen as successful reach within the target audience. • Identify the percentage of the total curriculum that was consumed by the targeted population on the specific topic, if any at all. • Inventory the manners in which the curriculum was distributed and what the reach and consumption was per distribution channel, if any previous content had been provided. • Investigate any patterns related to consumption. For example, time of day learners engaged with content or how much content was consumed in one sitting. • Examine any reported issues related to the initiative to determine its impact on reach or ability to complete the training curriculum.

Here again, try not to overwhelm the process by capturing everything, focus on one to two outcomes, and align 1–3 methods or pieces of information that can help evaluate the intended outcomes.

Marketing consultants strive to share their success because they know it will yield more business for them or their organization. The consultant and/or its organization are seen as credible and skilled. This is what IDs strive for with the work they do as well.

Conclusion

Integrating marketing practices and a consultative mindset to the instructional design process can lessen the effects of taking on project work that is driven by various requirements and constraints as opposed to strategically aligned outcomes. Focusing the client or project stakeholders on telling the story of their need will help the ID build a strategic profile that highlights opportunities and challenges in addressing the need.

Using common marketing categories to assess the impact of a training initiative provides a stronger pathway to strategic alignment, whether to the stakeholders or to the organization. Much like the diffusion of hybrid corn seed, these practices and methods may take time to be adopted by your ID team. However, experimentation in these practices will help to strengthen the consultative approach and influence conversations with your peers, the L&D department, and stakeholders.

Reference List

ATD Research. (2015, March). *Instructional design now: A new age of learning and beyond* [Whitepaper]. ATD. www.td.org/research/instructional-design-now.

Lowery, S.A., & DeFleur, M.L. (1995). *Milestones in mass communication research: Media effects* (3rd ed.). Longman Publishers.

Michaels, S. (2018, December 4). The L&D conundrum: Relevance or "order-taking"? *Training Industry.* https://trainingindustry.com/articles/professional-development/the-ld-conundrum-relevance-or-order-taking/

Out of the Frying Pan, Into the Fire

3

The Unintended (and Amazing) Consequences of Risk-Taking in the Practice of Instructional Design

Paul F. Desmarais M.ET.

Paul's Story

I never intended to be anything but a soldier. Until I didn't. I never intended to be anything other than a zoologist. Until I didn't. I never intended to be anything but a photojournalist. Until I didn't. Yet here I am, four decades into my adult life pursuing a career that was not even a viable option when I chose the army over college. Sir Ken Robinson said, many times, that universities are trying to prepare students for jobs that do not yet exist (2019). I know he was right, and I know it is possible because I am one of those students.

Each of the hairpin turns of my professional life has been accompanied by incredible experiences and inspiring relationships; each risk taken has inspired more risk-taking, regardless of the outcome. I have recently returned to the United States after working for two years in Egypt. As I was preparing to

DOI: 10.4324/9781003268413-3

36 Paul F. Desmarais

leave, a friend and former colleague questioned my sanity. Again. Three Vietnamese tourists were killed in a roadside bomb attack two weeks before I left for my new job. That same colleague called and suggested maybe I should do a rethink. He was not the only one. I got on that flight to Cairo, and I will always be glad I did.

As a former soldier, writer, photojournalist, and teacher I can say, without equivocation, the pursuit of excellence is a transferable skill. Persistence and resilience are transferable. Empathy developed interviewing a mother whose son was killed crossing a set of railroad tracks can be accessed when advising a university colleague on how to proceed after being racially abused by a superior. I have been able to mine the wisdom of colleagues from all of these different careers for the benefit of each and every one of the courses I designed, projects I led, programs I launched, and institutions I served. "Expect excellence, lieutenant, and that bunch of guys everyone thinks are nitwits will die trying to meet your expectations." Eddie DiPietro, my commanding officer said that to me when I was trying to raise the level of performance of a unit under my direction. I have used that lesson as a foundation for my approach to leadership and in the design of dozens of courses that integrate student-led activities.

With each change, each risk, comes new risks and new rewards. Thomas Jefferson, who took plenty of risks said, "With great risk comes great reward." Often, the risk is its own reward. Every leap into the unknown brings a sense of accomplishment and confidence as well as profound gratitude for all of the help that inevitably arrives from unexpected sources. My career path is not what anyone would call normal or typical, but I am able to bring what I learned in all of these other professions and contexts to bear for the benefit of legions of students who will never know I exist.

Risk & Risk-Taking as Important Elements in the Design of Instruction

Virtually every job posting in the field of instructional design will include phrases like these (Higher Ed Jobs, 2022):

- *Adept at identifying **innovative** online learning techniques . . .*
- *Skilled at **exploring emergent** technologies . . .*
- *Perform a regular **leadership** role . . .*
- *Experience with the following . . . **change management** . . .*

Out of the Frying Pan, Into the Fire **37**

Innovative, exploring, emergent, leadership, and change management are all words and phrases that suggest frequent, repeated, willful, and deliberate forays into the unknown.

According to various dictionary definitions, risk is "a situation involving exposure to danger." In business "risk is most commonly conceived as reflecting variation in the distribution of possible outcomes, their likelihoods, and their subjective values" (March & Shapira, 1987). The bottom line? People experience risk as fear of what *might* happen, fear of the unknown. For instructional designers, frequently, repeatedly, willfully, and deliberately plunging headlong into the unknown *is the job*. This means risk is an omnipresent part of the successful designer's reality. Risk, in other words, is both critical to success and an essential good (Hillson, 2001).

Rigidity in the Military vs. Higher Education

Instructional designers are people, and the reasons we avoid risks (which is often incorrectly equated with an absence of change) are the same reasons everyone else does; they are conditioned to do so. A study by Root, Inc. found that "67% of American employees can name at least one dynamic that would prevent them from taking any kind of risk at work" (Root, 2013).

Some of this is cultural. In the military, this takes the form of deference to the chain of command, rigid adherence to standard operating procedures (SOP), and a focus on punitive discipline. It is important to note that these are not the goals of the organizational structure in the military any more than in the hierarchy present in academia seeks to stifle innovation, but in the absence of good leadership, the structure reinforces itself, and institutions, like military commands, become rigid, inflexible, and incapable of innovation or change.

Risk avoidance looks very similar in both the military and academia.

The vertical authority structure and accountability models of most colleges and universities can act to stymie innovation (Findlow, 2008). Designers, like other employees, are conditioned to focus on their job responsibilities (stay in your lane) rather than looking for opportunities and innovations that might ruffle feathers.

Academia tends to reward "diplomatic decorum over radical candor." Academia frequently chooses a false sense of harmony over a diversity of ideas and critical feedback. In much the same way poor leaders in the military can opt for unquestioning obedience rather than input from subordinates. In either environment, this rigidity stifles the creativity of talented staff (like instructional designers) and leads to mediocre outcomes, not innovation (Vaughn, 2022).

Academia also prides itself on applying research-based approaches, which could be expressed as a *let's wait* versus a *let's go* mindset. Research takes time to do, time to analyze, and time to apply; all of which negatively impact the pace of innovation in the name of due diligence (aka risk aversion). In the military, this takes the form of kicking things up the chain of command, avoiding the risk that making a timely decision incurs.

PRACTICE ACTIVITY

Questions for Success

When faced with systemic rigidity in either the military or academia, a pathway to overcoming a stay-in-your-lane mentality might be found by asking a series of questions.

1. What is the source or root of the resistance? Stated differently, can I identify why the decision-maker is falling back on rigid hierarchy?
2. How do I link the innovation concretely and/or semantically to stated organizational goals?
3. What is the best way to I articulate the risks (and potential rewards) from resistant stakeholders' perspectives?

If you can answer these three questions, you can identify a pathway to success that risk-averse leaders can conceptualize and support.

Risk and Opportunity are Inextricably Connected

"In a world that's changing so quickly, the biggest risk you can take is not taking any risk." This is how billionaire venture capitalist Peter Thiel expressed the risk of not taking risks in a conversation with Mark Zuckerberg (Thiel, 2014). What Thiel is saying is that doing nothing and making changes both entail risk, but opportunity only exists by taking the risks associated with change.

The fact is risk exists whether we act or not. The risks of change are often similar to or even less than the risks of maintaining the status quo. Risk aversion does not result in safety and security but in lost opportunity, an absence of innovation, and careers stunted not by lack of ability but the fear of the unknown.

There are two aspects of risk that are poorly understood and incorrectly calculated. First is the myth that there is inherently more risk involved in change than maintaining the status quo. We are, as human beings and instructional designers, conditioned to believe this to be true. It is not.

The second myth about risk is that unknowns are likely to be bad and therefore, undesirable. Ergo, all risk is undesirable. The problem for instructional designers is that the prevalent definition of risk is unbalanced and incomplete. It also inhibits innovation. While the unknown is, in fact, uncertain, that uncertainty hides risk's undervalued but mission-critical cousin: opportunity (Sjöberg, 2003).

After I was commissioned, I was assigned to an artillery battery (a unit of about 110 people) as the assistant executive officer (AXO). I commanded a platoon (about 40 people). One of the units I inherited was a communications team of four soldiers. The team was unproductive, each member received below-average reviews on their performance evaluations for three straight years, and the former AXO and current platoon sergeant dealt with this underperformance by giving the team as little to do as possible to minimize the impact on the battery's performance. This approach worked in that the platoon met all its performance objectives. It failed in that the battery performance as a whole declined over five years from well above average to slightly below average. In this situation, there is a risk in doing nothing. Performance has been declining. There is risk in acting. The action might negatively impact performance. Things might get worse, but in reality, they already are. Performance is declining slowly but surely. So the risk in doing nothing is a slow, steady, assured decline. Opportunity exists only in taking action and assuming the risks that those actions carry.

In an instructional design context, there is a traditional face-to-face program that once enrolled 200 students, but in the five years since that peak, enrollment declined to 40 students. To date, the college has cut costs by reducing faculty and staff through attrition. From existing data, you can forecast that in five years the program will enroll too few students to be viable. When calculating the risk of change, it is more accurate to measure the risks of moving the program online in terms of having no program at all in five years as opposed to the perceived risk of losing a program that currently enrolls 40 students and considering those risks against the opportunity of enrolling the 100 additional students your market research forecasts.

40 Paul F. Desmarais

In both situations, there is no opportunity without change, but by failing to consider the opportunities as part and parcel of the risks, innovation and improvement are impossible.

Overcoming Risk Aversion

As an instructional designer, the pressure to maintain the status quo is often irresistible. We often hear this expressed as "If it ain't broke, don't fix it!" This rigid insistence that the status quo is better than and less risky than change is as stifling to innovation as it is incorrect. The challenge designers face is overcoming those biases to drive innovation, manage change, and create better, deeper, and more durable learning.

Howard Marks, the co-founder and co-chairman of Oaktree Capital Management, the largest investor in distressed securities worldwide said, "Risk control is the best route to loss avoidance. Risk avoidance, on the other hand, is likely to lead to return avoidance as well." What Marks is talking about is accurately assessing the positive/negative values of the risks, including those of *not* taking risks.

Tools for Overcoming Risk Aversion

One tool you can use to overcome risk aversion and be more innovative is recognizing the different biases that lead to creative paralysis. Here is a brief list of some of the most common reasons people avoid taking risks:

- Underestimating the risk of the status quo – the risks of change are thoroughly explored, but the risks of staying the course are not. With only the risks of change measured, organizations refuse to take "decisive action" (Martin, 2007).
- Installed base effect (bias) – The investment in terms of time and money in current technologies or systems serves as a barrier to replacement with a superior product or technology (Herbig & Kramer, 1993).
- Loss aversion – Fearing failure far more than valuing success (Vaughn, 2022).
- Narrow framing – A phenomenon where we weigh potential risks as if the outcomes of our projects exist in isolation as opposed to a larger strategy.
- Binary view – Risk is seen as a complete success or utter failure. The reality is that projects are part of a broader strategy, and the result of an

Out of the Frying Pan, Into the Fire 41

innovative approach is more likely to fall somewhere on a spectrum of outcomes, the vast majority being positive.

Together, these biases can reinforce the status quo in ways that are far more likely to be damaging to our institutions than a single failed project or projects (Koller et al., 2011).

It is important when discussing the risks of change to measure them and frame the conversation against the benefits and opportunities that change offers and measure the status quo in the same way – against the reality that the current state of being is neither risk-free nor inherently stable (Martin, 2007).

Another important tool that can drive innovation is the program or institutional adoption of performance standards. For example, a design environment where research-based quality standards have been established and best practices codified by the policy-level adoption of quality assurance tools like Quality Matters or the SUNY OSCQR rubric (at the course level) go a long way towards balancing the risk equation when designing online courses or programs. These standards help answer questions about online and hybrid course quality (Quality Matters, 2021).

It may seem like standards are the opposite of innovation, but most innovations build upon existing foundations. The modern wind turbine is innovative in that it creates electricity, while windmills of yore turned the wind into mechanical energy used to grind wheat into flour, pump water, and the like. A design standard allows the designer to take an innovation like student-managed groups discussions and relates them to a design standard like the OSCQR Rubric's #42, *Course offers opportunities for learner-to-learner interaction and constructive collaboration;* which can be tied to the third of Chickering and Gamson's Seven Principles for Good Practice in Undergraduate Education (Chickering & Gamson, 1987); "Encourage active learning."

Process is another tool for innovation that allows for repeatable excellence. On the face of it process, which speaks of manufacturing and routine, is often perceived as antithetical to innovation, but the opposite is true. The use of a process that, by design, includes quality assurance measures, helps ensure that an innovation will succeed, increasing the likelihood of adoption and that future innovations will be able to follow the same adoption pathway. Instructional design is itself, a process for the repeatable development of high-quality educational elements and environments (Dick et al., 2014).

Accepting the validity of diverse perspectives is another important tool in overcoming risk aversion in ourselves and others. Welcoming debate and criticism, helps overcome risk aversion because opposing viewpoints can

42 Paul F. Desmarais

highlight both risks and opportunities that a more homogenous perspective would miss. If an idea is worth the risk, it will hold up to rigorous challenges. Avoiding opposing viewpoints is a missed opportunity to improve, strengthen, and inform your ideas. Carl Sagan advised: "Encourage substantive debate on the evidence by knowledgeable proponents of all points of view." Accepting diverse and possibly dissenting viewpoints as valid allows discussion of the relative merit of the approaches, as opposed to a pro-forma acceptance or refusal based on the status quo, previous experience, or authority.

If we return to our earlier example, the poor performing communications team, we can apply these concepts to find ways to overcome the aversion to risks and act to improve the outcomes.

The first tool I used was performance standards, comparing the team's performance to the standards empirically. The communications unit, it turned out, had not always been so poor performing. At one point, it had been among the highest-performing units in the battery. The personnel were the same. The mission was the same. Why had the team's performance dropped? In conversations with the team members, they revealed that a change in leadership came with a demand to improve against the standard. One of the soldiers was frank; he just couldn't do what they wanted. He gave up. The second tool I used was soliciting diverse viewpoints. The soldiers themselves had a viewpoint on their performance. My former unit commander offered valuable insight. "Lieutenant, if you treat people like idiots, they'll live up to your expectations." He felt the current approach held more risk than any change I might initiate because what was going on now was not working and hadn't for three years. By tapping into the perspectives of others and using the standards and processes in place, I was able to initiate change confident that there was at a minimum, a better than fifty-fifty chance of dramatic improvement.

Finding Vision and Innovation in the Face of Risks

> To be an optimist is to embrace hope above all things.
>
> Winston Churchill

Churchill said that during the Battle of Britain. At the worst moment of World War II for the English, the prime minister, whether as a statement of politics or personal philosophy, articulated the successful instructional designer's creed.

To be an instructional designer requires this growth mindset, the same belief that it will be better next time, and the belief in the power of

Out of the Frying Pan, Into the Fire **43**

persistence and iterative development as Churchill articulated so profoundly in his nation's darkest hour.

The reality is that opportunity and risk are inherent in any action (or lack of action). If the status quo is the frying pan and risks associated with change are the fire, where a pessimist thinks, I'll get burned either way, an optimist learns to love the heat. To consistently lead, explore, innovate, or change, a designer has to learn to love the heat. Understanding risk in the context of opportunity and achievement allows designers to see risk as something to accept as inherent to every situation and as something to embrace as a twin sister to both opportunity and innovation.

Getting Buy-In: Semantics, Demonstration, and Culture

Overcoming risk aversion yourself turns out to be the easy part. As an instructional designer, you know that the core of the profession is collaboration. Virtually every project every designer has ever worked on, managed, led, or reviewed has been a collaboration with a member of the faculty, a subject matter expert, an administrator, or even a team involving a dozen or more people who all have to buy into the design for it to succeed.

Buy-in is important because in many cases, the perception of your design partner is that their current approach is succeeding. It is important to accept that this is a valid (if not necessarily correct) perspective. When a designer asks a SME with ten years of experience using an approach to teaching that they see as successful to change to something they have no direct experience of, it involves risk on the instructor's part (Gonzalez & Ozuna, 2021). The designer is asking them to put their professional reputation and their standing in the academic community on the line. Respecting that risk is essential to overcoming the conditioned aversion toward risking those things. The degree of buy-in will be dictated by how clearly, accurately, and confidently the designer communicates their assessment of the risks involved and the likelihood of success they can forecast.

Communicating Your Vision – Semantics

Establishing a concrete, readily discernible connection between the existing state and the context you are transferring knowledge *from* to the one you are transferring *into* by using the same language. For example, when you discuss something as simple as a unit of instruction, what word do you use? Module?

44 Paul F. Desmarais

Unit? Chapter? Week? When you are trying to formulate the end products of instruction, how do you describe them? Do you express them as goals, objectives, learning outcomes, or competencies? Many academics use these terms interchangeably, but for instructional designers, these terms have specific meanings; they and the SME, faculty member, or design team members are all using them to mean the same things. These may seem like minor points; after all, we're innovating! But language is how we communicate and using the same language means you have a shared understanding of everything, including any risks involved.

Avoidance of jargon whenever possible is important, as is establishing a common tongue for design discussions. This is accomplished by asking the right questions. Do you and your partner agree on the project goals and parameters? How does your partner teach? Why do they teach that way? What are their experiences? Asking questions and then connecting your prior experiences and their prior experiences with this new context semantically will go a long way to getting the buy-in necessary to overcome a partner's aversion to taking risks with an innovative design.

Demonstration

When your faculty partner says, "You can't teach chemistry online," don't dispute the statement; *show* how it can be done. I worked as an instructional designer for an engineering school designing courses in space systems, electrical, and environmental engineering, as well as applied mathematics. In a subsequent position, I was told by numerous instructors that it was impossible to teach engineering or math well online. Since I had already designed high-quality online engineering and mathematics instruction and seen faculty at my prior institution deliver it, I was certain it was not only possible but done routinely. The issue was not who was right and who was wrong, but the personal experience and scope of pedagogical knowledge of the people involved in the conversation.

Telling instructor-experts that "It's possible, I've done it." is not an effective technique for three reasons. First, the designer is, in effect, saying they know something the SME does not, which can be insulting even if (perhaps especially if) true. Second, *telling* does not provide the necessary context within which instructor-experts can build their own knowledge. Finally, arguing from authority is rarely effective. Experts and authorities (even instructional designers!) have been and will continue to be wrong (Sagan, 1997).

Successfully transferring lived experience to this project meant modeling success. Taking specific, successful models of assignments, assessments, and so on and sharing them, making clear connections with faculty members' own pedagogical experiences (discovered by asking them), demonstrated that it could and has been done within a similar instructional context by faculty with a similar level of skill and experience.

Culture

There is a sense that innovation is all about change, and it is (Hall, 2021). That change, for instructional designers at least, occurs within a very specific framework: the company, organization, or institution that employs them. Each college, university, government agency, or company will have certain characteristics that define them and together form an institutional culture. That culture is what drives the behaviors of individuals who will innovate (or not). According to business strategist, Willis Towers Watson (WTW) the interweaving of strategy and culture is so complete that the alignment of the two is essential for successful innovation (change). Working within as opposed to against institutional norms is comforting to design partners and provides an established context for the associated change or risks.

Being Successful – Adopting a Growth Mindset

A growth mindset can be distilled down to a single word: yet. We have not reached our enrollment goals . . . yet. We have not delivered all 16 planned courses in this program . . . yet. It is not about accepting failure but looking at the present as a single point on a continual timeline of constant change. In the context of risk-taking, adopting a growth mindset is about embracing optimism and risk as essential to improvement. It is about acknowledging challenges and meeting them through persistence (Nicholson, 2008).

A growth mindset in the context of design innovation means embracing risk and accepting the possibility (not the inevitability) of failure as a natural part of change. For a designer, a growth mindset means accepting negative feedback as an essential tool for professional growth and keeping it in context. "This did not work this time" as opposed to "This does not work!" Learning to be comfortable with taking measured risks is essential to embracing growth and change as a baseline of a creative existence; and what is an instructional designer if not a creator?

46 Paul F. Desmarais

Reflection – A Driver of Successful Risk-Taking

With successful innovation as a goal, reflection is a powerful tool in achieving it and the excellence in learning that follows. Educational psychologist, John Dewey describes reflection.

> Reflection involves not simply a sequence of ideas, but a consequence – a consecutive ordering in such a way that each determines the next as its proper outcome, while each in turn leans back on its predecessors.

When we use reflection to mine prior knowledge, examine performance and inform decisions, it is the desired consequences that must be the focus. We use reflection to connect specific actions with the consequences of taking those actions and draw enough parallels when communicating the fruit of our reflections for our SMEs or faculty partners to conclude that the same results can be reasonably predicted from similar actions in our new (innovative) instructional context (Dewey, 1910).

When reflecting on the success that trusting my communications team soldiers yielded, I focused on the desired consequences: clearly defined, realistic, improved performance that was framed within the established cultural norms of the organization. Reflection is perhaps the most powerful tool any single individual has to inform their success, but it is most effective when the reflection is reframed within Dewey's ordering, outcome, predecessor, and consequences framework.

PRACTICE ACTIVITY

Seeking an Outside Perspective

It can be a challenge to reflect alone, in which case an outside perspective can help shed light on your intended plan and whether or not it needs to be modified. Getting an outside perspective can help you reflect on aspects of your plan that you didn't see at first.

1. Identify individuals with similar skill levels to those you are trying to develop a plan for
2. Present the proposed plan with as much detail as possible

3. Solicit feedback asking for both pros, cons, and possible reactions to the proposed plan
4. Reflect on the feedback
5. Modify the plan, if necessary, in order to obtain the desired outcome

It's important to work with individuals who are in similar positions to the individuals you are trying to support. With "no skin in the game," they will be able to look at your ideas objectively, and their input and perspectives are more likely to be relevant than those of more senior or experienced leaders because they have similar capacities and similar skills as you.

Accountability – The Final Word in a Risk-Taking Strategy

Like the military, educational institutions are rooted in accountability. Colleges and universities are steeped in practices and language associated with personal and professional responsibility. Nearly every institution has a policy regarding academic integrity, for example. The very core of how institutions measure student achievement – assessment of student learning – is accountability for performance expressed as a percentage of the possible. This accountability is what allows institutions to certify achievement by the awarding of degrees.

Aligning risk-taking with accountability encourages innovation in much the same way aligning assessment with objectives encourages ownership. When an individual is empowered to take measured risks and is willing to accept responsibility for their decisions, regardless of the outcome, it creates a sense of ownership and autonomy in much the same way that fostering learner autonomy is directly related to a sense of ownership of a student's education and correlated directly with academic success. The critical piece of this is that the ownership and accountability are transparent and align with the risk (Moore, 2017).

Successful risk-taking and the innovation it drives must be recognized in proportion to how it improves the organization, and any failure must be equally aligned and not given more weight than any damage to the organization. Too often one small failure is given enormous weight relative to successful innovations.

Accountability also allows for the development of resilience. If a strategy fails, an individual can accept responsibility and move on rather than dwell on any single failure and become mired in counterproductive finger-pointing designed to assign blame.

PRACTICE ACTIVITY

What If?

A strategy you can use in nearly every scenario you encounter as a designer is "What if?" This will help you reflect on the risks and whether or not you are willing to be accountable for any potential outcomes. To engage in this activity, you simply ask, "What if?" and try to anticipate what might happen in the situation. Here are a few example questions:

- What if I do nothing?
- What if the approach fails?
- What if this works as I expect?

By reflecting on the potential results of different actions and non-actions, you can make decisions and your accountability for a given set of actions and outcomes.

Conclusion

To be an instructional designer is to learn to accept risk, embrace it, to learn to love the heat. It requires the same optimism Churchill articulated so profoundly in his nation's darkest hour. This is not a Pollyana sentiment. Instructional designers, like painters, dancers, and sculptors create something that did not previously exist and could not exist without them. Look at the last course you designed and compare it to one the same instructor taught the semester before. Would you or the students, or the instructor prefer the previous version?

Instructional design is intensely detail-oriented, requiring focus and above all, a view of risk as an essential good. To be an instructional designer is to be a process-oriented technocrat capable of leading a complex project, an

Out of the Frying Pan, Into the Fire **49**

open-minded intellectual capable of engaging in an andragogical debate with a tenured rhetorician, and a strategic thinker capable of assessing risk and forecasting success like a crisis manager. Anyone who can do all that can change the world. You probably already have.

Reference List

Chickering, W.A., & Gamson, F.Z. (1987). Seven principles for good practice in undergraduate education. *The American Association for Higher Education (AAHE) Bulletin.*

Davey, L. (2014). The status quo is risky too. *The Harvard Business Review.* https://hbr.org/2014/05/the-status-quo-is-risky-too

Dewey, J. (1910). *How we think.* Heath.

Dick, W., Carey, L., & Carey, J. (2014). *The systematic design of instruction* (8th ed.). Pearson.

Ertmer, P.A., Stepich, D.A., York, C., Wu, X., Zurek, S., & Goktas, Y. (2008). How instructional design experts use knowledge and experience to solve ill-structured problems. *Performance Improvement Quarterly, 21*(1), 17–42.

Findlow, S. (2008). Accountability and innovation in higher education: A disabling tension? *Studies in Higher Education, 33*(3), 313–329. https://doi.org/10.1080/03075070802049285

Gonzalez, L., & Ozuna, C.S. (2021). Troublesome knowledge: Identifying barriers to innovate for breakthroughs in learning to teach online. *Online Learning, 25*(3), 81–96. https://doi.org/10.24059/olj.v25i3.2641

Hall, M. (2021). The power of culture in navigating climate-related risks and opportunities. *Willis Towers Watson.* www.wtwco.com/en-US/Insights/2021/09/the-power-of-culture-in-navigating-climate-related-risks-and-opportunities

Herbig, P.A., & Kramer, H. (1993). The power of the installed base. *Journal of Business and Industrial Marketing, 8*(3), 44–57.

Higher Ed Jobs. (2022). Director of Distance Education. www.higheredjobs.com/admin/details.cfm?JobCode=177767377&Title=Director%20of%20Distance%20Education

Hillson, D. (2001). *Effective strategies for exploiting opportunities.* Paper presented at Project Management Institute Annual Seminars & Symposium. Project Management Institute.

Kirschner, P.A., Carr, C., van Merringboer, J., & Sloep, P. (2008). How expert designers design. *Performance Improvement Quarterly, 15*(4). Wiley online library. https://doi.org/10.1111/j.1937-8327.2002.tb00267.x

Koller, T., Lovallo, D., & Williams, Z. (2011). *Overcoming a bias against risk. Corporate finance practice.* McKinsey & Co.

March, J.G., & Shapira, Z. (1987). Managerial perspectives on risk and risk taking. *Management Science, 33*(11), INFORMS, 1404–1418. www.jstor.org/stable/2631920

Martin, R. (2007). *Underestimating the risk of the status quo.* Rotman Magazine.

Moore, J. (2017). Supporting innovation with autonomy and accountability. *Innovation Management,* January 17. Retrieved from: https://innovationmanagement.se/2017/01/30/innovation-autonomy-accountability/

Nicholson, L. (2008). *Adopting a growth mindset: How your attitudes about failure can determine your success.* Linked In. https://www.linkedin.com/pulse/adopting-growth-mindset-how-your-attitudes-failure-can-nicholson

Quality Matters. (2021). *Specific review standards from the QM higher education rubric* (6th ed.). Quality Matters. www.qualitymatters.org/qa-resources/rubric-standards/higher-ed-rubric

Robinson, K., & Robinson, K. (2019). *Imagine If: Creating a future for us all*. Penguin

Root Inc. (2013, March 26). *New study reveals what U.S. employees really think about today's workplace*. GlobeNewswire News Room. https://www.globenewswire.com/news-release/2013/03/26/1079193/0/en/New-Study-Reveals-What-U-S-Employees-Really-Think-About-Today-s-Workplace.html

Sagan, C. (1997). *The demon-haunted world: Science as a candle in the dark*. Penguin.

Sjöberg, L. (2003). The different dynamics of personal and general risk. *Risk Management, Palgrave Macmillan Journals, 5*(3), 19–34. www.jstor.org/stable/3867764

SUNY Online Course Quality Review Rubric: OSCQR. https://oscqr.suny.edu/

Thiel, P. (2014). *Zero to one: Notes on startups, or how to build the future*. Crown.

Vaughn, T. (2022). 3 ways a culture of risk avoidance limits growth. *Forbes*.

Critical Theory for Critical Work

4

Feminist Approaches to Instructional Design

Jaclyn Dudek

Jackie's Story

This chapter is devoted to developing feminist approaches to instructional design by drawing on the wider concepts and themes of feminist thought across disciplines. Feminist pedagogy and values already make up essential parts of our instructional design practice. Still, feminist approaches in instructional design remain implicit at best, and instructional designers are often disconnected from broader theoretical discussions within the fields of education and design. Although technical skill is still an essential part of our expertise, much of our work is based on building relationships, advocating for learners, and for fair and ethical practices from our organizations and institutions. Instructional designers already incorporate aspects of feminist pedagogy and design into our practice. We just need to admit it.

Ursula K. Le Guin, fantasy novelist, and feminist author wrote a wondrous little gem of an essay called *The Carry Bag of Theory of Fiction*. It is a short read, and if you get anything out of this chapter, it might be that essay. From

DOI: 10.4324/9781003268413-4

52   Jaclyn Dudek

this, I borrow both her metaphor and argument to explore the idea of developing a feminist approach to instructional design.

Le Guin builds upon anthropologist Elizabeth Fisher's (1979) theory that the first cultural device was probably a receptacle, such as a pouch, net, or bag rather than some sort of implement of violence (i.e., the spear). The history of primates and birds using tools such as sticks, straws, or pokers to get at food is well documented. A pokey stick is not only a human thing. But a bag, a bottle, a basket, that's something altogether different. According to Le Guin and Fisher, the bag or receptacle is a uniquely human cultural tool. A receptacle is used to save things for later and move things to and fro.

> If it is a human thing to do to put something you want, because it's useful, edible, or beautiful, into a bag, or a basket, or a bit of rolled bark or leaf, or a net woven of your own hair, or what have you, and then take it home with you, home being another, larger kind of pouch or bag, a container for people, and then later on you take it out and eat it or share it or store it up for winter in a solider container or put it in the medicine bundle or the shrine or the museum, the holy place, the area that contains what is sacred, and then next day you probably do much the same again.
>
> (Le Guin, 1986)

The essay proceeds to investigate this more feminist perspective on technology and Le Guin's own genre of science fiction. The transmission of culture was not via the sword, spear, or plow (all phallic metaphors) but through the technology of the bag (womb metaphors abounding). Le Guin also investigates and rejects the traditional concept of the hero within novels. For this discussion, let's focus on the bag.

> Once you think about it, surely long before – the weapon, a late, luxurious, superfluous tool; long before the useful knife and ax; right along with the indispensable whacker, grinder, and digger – for what's the use of digging up a lot of potatoes if you have nothing to lug ones you can't eat home in – with or before the tool that forces energy outward, we made the tool that brings energy home. It makes sense to me.
>
> (Le Guin, 1986)

The first time I read Le Guin's essay, it resonated on many levels. I am a bag woman myself, meaning that I always have too much to carry and not enough bags to schlep around all of my things. I have lots of digital bags too in the form of computers, a phone, and several email accounts. I am also a gardener and gatherer (another topic described in the essay) and as such have an appreciation for how and when to gather and store the things you find or have grown by putting them in special containers. For example, cucumbers in a jar with a few extra ingredients and time can easily be turned into pickles.

On subsequent readings, this carrier bag metaphor has increasingly occupied my imagination. If it served useful to understand feminist science fiction writing, why not feminist instructional design? I argue that at the most fundamental level our professional practice is to make containers to transport, hold, and nurture learning and information. We organize, design, and caringly wrap learning so that it is transportable and usable for the learner when they need it. We help shuttle competencies and skills, and hard-fought wisdom across time and space. When people demand the newest, shiniest, pokey stick, we calmly ask them, *Do you need a bag for that*? As instructional designers, we are all bag people.

Think about it.

Introduction

Being a feminist is different from being a feminist theorist. Indeed, the two are bound together. Someone who identifies as a feminist might personally espouse certain political and social values and beliefs, most notably the discrepancies in health, economic, and political agency of women. Being a feminist scholar means systematically working across feminist a) content and contexts (centering on the topics described above), b) forms of inquiry (the types of questions asked), and c) research and design (methods, artifacts, and solutions). Although gender is an essential lens through which feminists try to understand the world, it is not the only one. At its heart, feminist theories strive to:

* Understand and change how power is situated
* Privilege and elevate multiple perspectives and ways of knowing
* Attend to and honor lived experiences, emotions, and embodiment as important sources for learning and knowledge

This chapter explains what feminist theories *can do* for instructional design. I hope to impart how thinking with critical theories, feminist theories being one of many, is vital to our work. Critical theories are not tools

54 Jaclyn Dudek

for our professional toolbox. Instead, they are lenses to focus and reshape our experience with the world. Taking a feminist approach lays out how we shift our attention from spears to bags and understand the implications of doing so.

Critical Theory for Critical Work

Instructional design work is fundamentally political. I don't mean political as in governmental parties, but political in that instructional designers deeply engage with and often question socio-cultural and economic practices where knowledge and learning are forms of power. Instructional designers are not (and never have been) objective technocrats. Instead, instructional designers are reflexive experts who must move fluidly through institutions to ultimately do right by our learners.

Instructional designers constantly leverage the practical with the ethical and pedagogical. We deal with fundamentally political and power-based questions: *"What should be learned?"* and *"How should it be organized?"* The first is a question of political *content*, the second is a question of political *form* (Petrina, 2004). To this I add a third question, "What is the role of the user within the design," which is a question of political *agency*. Instructional designers often hold essential roles as change agents within organizations because we facilitate how these questions get asked and how they are answered. Instructional designers are important facilitators of these power-infused discussions, whether we like it or not. Because of these roles and responsibilities, I argue that instructional designers need to engage more with critical theories to understand, critique, or expand the various roles, design methods, and forms of educational change that instructional designers shape. Critical digital pedagogy scholar-practitioners like Jesse Strommel, co-founder of the online journal Hybrid Pedagogy, echo my own sentiment that claiming a kind of political neutrality for the work we do is impossible. "Educators and students alike have found themselves more and more flummoxed by a system that values assessment over engagement, learning management over discovery, content over the community, outcomes over epiphanies. Education (and, to an even greater extent, edtech) has misrepresented itself as objective, quantifiable, apolitical" (Strommel, 2012).

Thus, questions like *who gets to learn, when,* and *where,* take on increased political consequences as they expose inequities in our society. These are also questions that instructional designers tackle every day. Feminist theories, provide a constellation of guiding principles, practices, and values that support instructional designers in our work by providing vocabularies, methods, and modes of inquiry for understanding and addressing these questions and challenges.

What Is the Role of Theory?

Feminist theory, from an academic perspective, describes a system of methods, questions, ethical values, and political perspectives that examines the economic, social, political, and psychological position of women. Earlier feminist approaches sought to critique oppressive power structures and single totalizing narratives of women and other marginalized people. Feminist theory has transformed social sciences, including; law (Crenshaw, 1990), education (Ladson-Billings, 1998; hooks, 2003), and technology studies (Haraway, 1988; Sørensen, 2009). Similarly, Feminist theory informs qualitative research methods (Pink, 2008; St. Pierre, 1997), design-based (Costanza-Chock, 2018) and human-computer interaction design [HCI] (Bardzell, 2010), and more recently, data science and quantitative research methods (D'Ignazio & Klein, 2020). For example, design justice is a field of theory and practice that is concerned with how the design of objects and systems influences the distribution of risks, harms, and benefits among various groups of people. Design justice focuses on the ways that designs reproduce or challenge the dominant norms (Costanza-Chock, 2018). I believe that we all care about ethical and inclusive designs. When given the chance, instructional designers tend to challenge the status quo rather than comply with it. We are the quiet rebels. Us and those riotous librarians.

Let's return to our bag discussion to put this into perspective. Just as the carrier bag theory of civilization cannot be proved or disproved, feminist theories give us a lens or perspective to work with. Shifting perspectives means that we are able to explore different values, tools, and beliefs. Therefore, it is not finding something new, but rather paying attention to things that we normally don't. I argue that feminist concepts, pedagogies, and design approaches can help focus and elevate vocabularies, positionalities, and practices to instructional design. It's all there, we just need to pay attention to it. In this chapter I explore four feminist concepts: intersectionality, positionality, reflexivity, and embodiment. Based on the work of *Data Feminism* (D'Ignazio & Klein, 2020) I offer six principles of feminist instructional design and how they can be applied to our work in big and small ways.

56 Jaclyn Dudek

Feminist Theory's Impact on Instructional Design Practice

More than twenty years ago, Carr, Jonassen, Litzinger, and Marra outlined several shifts that needed to happen for feminist pedagogy to gain a foothold in learning environments. The first shift was to accept learners as a personal authority in addition to (or instead of) the teacher as a singular expert. The second is recognizing how the affective domain influences learning and the construction of knowledge. Finally, education needs to be reframed from a competitive process to a framework for growth and self-reflection (Carr et al., 1998). Based on these criteria, instructional designers already work in learning environments where feminist pedagogy is the norm.

At the same time, there has been a disconnect between broad pedagogical positions with technology and the ethical collection and use of learner data. For example, conversations around technologies primarily emphasize the "economic utility" of tools for speed or efficiency rather than learning (Amiel & Reeves, 2008). Questions of learner agency are often ignored in favor of the "ethic of expediency, which often drives technology design" (Salvo, 2001, p. 276). Because technology is incorporated in all aspects of our lives, people must also be empowered to conscientiously evaluate the role of technology in their learning and teaching. Technology is not value neutral. Similarly, as D'Ignazio & Klein have shown, algorithms and data sets are products of assumption, biases, and often repeat if not magnify inequalities (2020). For this reason, designers need to be versed in critical conversations arounds the collection and use of data, the design and development of tools and artifacts, and the larger learning environment. The next section describes the concepts that support feminist instructional design principles, intersectionality, positionality and reflexivity, and embodiment. Across the discussion, I describe the people that interact with our designs as users to encompass learners, educators, administrators, or others who are directly impacted by our designed learning systems.

Intersectionality

Intersectional thinking, intersectional design, and intersectional pedagogy help us understand people's complex identities and relations. Intersectionality came out of legal theory around anti-discrimination and is an important concept within critical race theory (Crenshaw, 1990, 2017). Intersectionality describes the various identities or positionalities that individuals may hold

Critical Theory for Critical Work **57**

(like religion) or be ascribed (like race). The interconnected nature of social categorization, such as race, class, and gender create overlapping and interdependent disadvantage or privilege systems. Crenshaw describes intersectionality as less of a grand theory and more as a prism to understand different questions. For our discussion, I focus on a more generative use of the term to understand the impact of our designs and the lived reality of our users.

Understanding thick intersectionality supports a more nuanced and productive discussion of diversity, equity, and inclusive learning environments. Knowing *what* our users are (demographics, task analysis, etc.) is an important part of the design process. However, it is also important to know *who* our users are too (Stefaniak & Baaki, 2013). Designers can use personas to explore user archetypes. Nevertheless, it is equally important to listen to personal narratives to understand our users' hopes, dreams, aspirations, and fears. Stefaniak and Baaki's layered approach to understanding users (2013) serves as a helpful guide for developing our intersectional observations. Other examples of operationalizing such an approach can be found in frameworks like identity-centered design (Dudek & Heiser, 2017) and inclusive teaching and course design (Gamrat, 2020).

PRACTICE ACTIVITY

Engaging With Intersectional Thinking and Design

Representation matters; users need to see themselves and others in their learning environments.

- Review readings and resources. What percentage of textbooks, articles, and videos are authored or feature the voices of people of color, women, international scholars (from the global south).
- When using historical examples, research/include lesser known but still extraordinary people.
- Do learning scenarios and examples depict or make visible diverse relationships and diverse family structures?
- Do learning scenarios and examples offer strength-based depictions of people with disabilities (visible and not visible)?

Users have lives beyond the classroom or workplace. Without disrespecting people's privacy, allow for more fluidity to bring other parts of people's lives to their learning. Designers can leverage users' intersectionality to create supportive learning environments.

- Users learn with others. This means pets, children, parents, siblings, spouses, and colleagues.
- Users learn (and sometimes work) while doing other life things like eating, exercising, and commuting.
- Users are caretakers. They might take care of their siblings, their own children, parents, and family members.
- Users are community members. They participate in and are active in communities of faith, geography, and interests.
- Users are from different geographical areas that impact their culture, access, and proximity to resources.

Ask intersectional questions and look for patterns within different overlapping demographics and scenarios. Looking for outliers can provide insight into those who follow the general pattern.

- Who is in the learning environment to begin with? Are there bottlenecks? Who is overrepresented and why? Is overrepresentation a good thing?
- Who succeeds in the current learning environment and why?
- Who struggles and why?
- Who do we struggle to retain and why?

Positionality and Reflexivity

The feminist concepts of *positionality* and *reflexivity* support the iterative practices of inquiry and critique. In her talk, *Design Thinking is Bullsh*t*, designer Natasha Jen criticizes the simplification and commercialization of the designing process to linear steps in the form of hexagons and Post-its (2018). Jen argues that the commonly used design thinking models lull us into a linear expectation rather than an iterative cycle. Criticism – an integral part of the design process – spurs iteration and the feedback cycle – is missing from the equation. When I reflect on my experiences with design thinking, lots of time was spent trying to understand the user. There was never an opportunity to explore my relationship with the users whom I was designing for. My identity, experience, bias, distance, or proximity were never considered. Self-critique

Critical Theory for Critical Work **59**

can only take one so far. Qualitative research traditions and feminist pedagogy influence my treatment of positionality and reflexivity.

Linda Alcoff first introduced the idea of positionality, which is how individuals come to the knowledge making process from multiple positions, and each is determined by culture and context (1991). Positionalities are the identities we hold (i.e., race, language, or gender) and the experiences (or lack thereof) that we bring to situations. Positionalities are often relational; their meaning is derived in relationship with other identities and roles. Some positionalities can be chosen, such as the decision to come to a situation or learning context as a practitioner with one set of heuristics and strategies rather than with the perspective of a researcher, which evokes a different set of concerns and skills. Sometimes positionality can be attenuated, being turned up or down as the context or objective calls for. Other positionalities cannot be chosen, and the awareness of these positions are not always empowering. DuBois' *double consciousness* and Anzaldúa's concept of *nepantla* (1987) are examples of how critical theorists have wrestled with understanding their own positionalities in relation to wider cultural and political forces.

Reflexivity is the process of being aware of our positionalities, assumptions, and biases. It is different from being reflective. Feminist scholar Wanda Pillow provides a distinction, "Being reflective does not demand an 'other,' while to be reflexive demands both an 'other' and some self-conscious awareness on the process of self-scrutiny" (Pillow, 2003). Another way to describe reflexivity is by critical pedagogue Paulo Freire's conception of praxis as compared to practice. Praxis is the "reflection and action upon the world in order to transform it" (1970, p. 51). Reflexivity is a transformational process that considers and anticipates failures as well as success in that the goal is not to be objective or eliminate bias but rather to transform our understandings and assumptions. Furthermore, reflexivity acknowledges that there will always be a blind spot(s) during this transformative process, requiring more communication and checking in by all stakeholders and pushing back against stakeholders when necessary. In short, practice and reflection are processes that are inherently focused inward. They are helpful at developing technical or personal skill that are not relational. On the other hand, praxis and reflexivity are focused outward and require an understanding of community within an institution, organization of disciplinary field, and the desire to change those institutions on a structural level.

In this section, I intentionally conflate critique as design practice and using critical theoretical stances to make a larger point. Designing with feminist concepts is one way to engage in the critique process. Positionality describes how various identities may be invoked in various situations. The identities

60   Jaclyn Dudek

we hold both effect and affect knowledge building, power dynamics, and how others view us as insiders or outsiders. Understanding how our positionalities are relational and dynamic to contexts supports more empathetic, inclusive, and resilient learning environments.

PRACTICE ACTIVITY

Ways to engage with positionality and reflexivity:

How would you describe your praxis, who has it changed and who/ what are you influenced by?

- Write a design philosophy statement. It can be as long or short as you see fit but it should try to answer the following;
  - o Understanding who I am, where I do come from, and where I'm at currently
  - o Describe what you believe are the core human/learning needs for users to be successful and thrive
  - o Align personal values with your work
  - o Describe your go-to learning and activity models, how do they speak to you, and why
  - o Describe how you adapt and compromise
  - o Outline your core guiding design principles

Where do you come from, biases, proclivities, and all?

- For those who are creatively and aesthetically minded, the writer and teacher George Ella Lyons (http://www.georgeellalyon. com/) has adapted a template format of her poem, Where I'm From. I have used this in lieu or in addition to having colleagues and students write a more traditional academic or professional positionality statement. I like this activity because it reveals something about a designer's aesthetics.

Build in space for critique by adopting a studio approach with informal critique sessions.

- According to Hoadley and Cox (2008), "the paradox of teaching design is that designers know things, but they can't tell others about them in a way that novices will understand" (p. 19). Adopting a design studio approach with informal "crits" from peers and other experts can build these constructive critiquing skills and also explore multiple perspectives (Hokanson, 2020)

The following critique and reflection prompts are based on Lacheb and Boling (2021) work on developing design judgments.

- Choose a focus for the critique —a challenge with a designer, a moment of design failure, a disagreement with a SME, a personal tension, etc.
- Describe your design actions by addressing the Five W's (What, When, Where, Why, Who).
- Focus and elaborate on the "Why" part so you can reveal the design judgments you made that led to these design actions.
- Draw upon your positionality and reflexivity and be honest about biases or lack of understanding, the "Why" when speaking about others' actions.

Embodiment

There are many ways to define embodiment within feminist theory. In general, embodiment explores the idea that there is a vital relationship of the lived body – the materiality of skin, bone, and breath in motion – to thought, to knowledge, and to ethics. Here, I posit two ways that instructional designers can benefit from this feminist theme. First, embodiment decenters the notion that thinking only happens in the head and that the body is a convenient way of moving our brain computers around. Our entire body is engaged in sense and meaning-making or what learning scientists describe as embodied cognition (Lakoff, 2012). Emotion and embodiment are entangled just as thinking and feeling. We have a desperate need to create learning environments where users feel safe physically and emotionally. For users who are neurodiverse and process sensory input differently, embodiment is a key understanding to support their physical and mental well-being.

Second, embodiment provides a lens to analyze and rectify how different bodies have been treated, designed for, and excluded. In Le Guin's essay, she describes this phenomenon to some extent both in bodies and through the lens

62 Jaclyn Dudek

of novels and the genre of fiction. Feminist embodiment considers how bodies have historically been categorized as not normal or deviant. Such deviant bodies have generally been the bodies of women, people of color, intersexed, and disabled people. Shaowen Bardzell, a HCI scholar, calls for designers to look first at those outside the standard experience. Bardzell argues that starting with people at the margins in a design context demonstrates *who* and *what* the system is trying to exclude. Feminist design approaches in HCI compliments the instructional design community's advocation for accessible educational technologies by arguing that bringing designs into ADA compliance is only the bare minimum (Bardzell, 2010). Another scholar and activist, Alice Wong's Disability Visibility Project [DVP] supports "an online community dedicated to sharing, amplifying disability media and culture" and provides educators, activists, artists, and scholars resources for reframing notions of disability and showcasing different media and designs (https://disabilityvisibilityproject.com/about/). Instructional designers and accessibility specialists advocate that accessibility is at the forefront of design decisions rather than retrofitting something at the end of the design process.

Increasingly, instructional designers work with hybrid worlds where the environment is fully immersive [VR] or augmented [AR] by technology, which necessitates being highly attuned to how people learn with their body. Instructional designers need to engage in learning theories of embodied cognition and situated learning to design authentic tasks and assessments for users. Whether designing for a complex nursing simulation or an accessible website that all users can read and navigate, embodiment helps us remember to pay attention to how the tools we use and places we inhabit affect the body. Finally, embodiment helps us recognize that all work has its own complexities and expertise.

PRACTICE ACTIVITY

Engaging with Embodiment

- Where are users' bodies within the learning environment or learning duration? We don't sit to learn. We sit to *record* the learning, usually by typing on a keyboard, writing on paper, or recording ourselves sitting and talking into a microphone. Learning is a movement from one state to another. Focus on where the body is during the learning episode; how is it moving and what materials are alongside it? Is there enough light, air, and space?

- Are learning tools accessible for differently abled people (sight, sound, keyboard shortcuts)?
- Are learning spaces accessible and welcoming for differently abled people?
- Are users learning in tandem with other activities, such as driving, cooking, exercising, for example? Can these embedded co-activities be leveraged as part of the learning or variables to contend with? Multiple modalities provide learner flexibility as they learn on the go as part of their multitasking lives.
- What are the ways bodies know what our minds do not or language cannot express? How can we leverage the understanding that bodies are learning instruments?
- Trauma lives in the body. For those interested in trauma informed pedagogy, it is essential to understand how the body reacts and heals from stress. Learning can act as a trigger or a form of healing.
- What learning materials can we collect or design that supports rich embodied cues, like touch, sound, color, or smell?
- Consider making data and information visceral – something that can be felt physically or emotionally.

Incorporating Feminist Theory Into Instructional Design Practices

Instructional designers occupy an intersectional role within organizations and institutions. I advocate that we must engage with critical theories and learning theories as a field of academic research and professional practice. While many other feminist concepts could be explored, intersectionality, positionality, reflexivity, and embodiment contribute to instructional design theory and practice. When instructional designers work intentionally with these concepts, we strive to make our designs more equitable. Therefore, instructional designers cannot take a neutral or objective position when designing learning environments and systems.

To operationalize the agenda above, I offer the following six feminists principles for instructional design, based on the work of D'Ignazio and Klein in their book *Data Feminism* (2020).

1. **Examine and challenge power:** How do power and agency operate in the organizational/learning system. How do we recognize unequal and unfair power structures (implicit or explicit) and challenge them with action?
2. **Elevate emotion and embodiment**: Feminist instructional design values multiple forms of knowledge, including the knowledge that comes from living and feeling bodies.
3. **Embrace pluralism:** The most comprehensive knowledge is derived from multiple modalities, perspectives, and pedagogies, prioritizing collaborative and experiential ways of knowing.
4. **Consider the context**: Data is not neutral. Technology/tools are not neutral or objective. Often, the content is not neutral. Since our designs synthesize these elements, they are products of (possibly unequal) social relations.
5. **Make labor visible:** This has two parts: 1) instructional design is an interdisciplinary field and collaborative practice. We work with educators, librarians, subject matter experts, media experts, technologists, and programmers. The implementation of our designs is the work of many hands. Feminist instructional design approaches strive to make this labor visible to be recognized and valued. 2) Making labor visible also means making expertise and skill visible. When designing systems and training, pay attention to and don't underestimate entry-level employees/learners. The people who have the most insight into how jobs and tasks are done by the people who do them – not managers or high-level employees.
6. **Ethical use of learner data, analytics, and tools:** Many tools have surveillance capabilities, from social media to learning management system. Similarly, given the well-publicized representation issues in Silicon Valley, we need to engage in more critique of the privilege and experiences of the creators and the resulting biases evident in the technology. Consider asking critical questions when choosing technology tools, which often comes at great expense to the institution, learners or employees. Who developed this product? Who is profiting from this product and how?

Conclusion

Feminist theory is not a unifying theory about women, females, or gender. Instead, feminist theory is a constellation of concepts, methods, and values that examines how power is situated and knowledge is created. As a professional and academic field, we do not need more instructional design models. Instead, we need to intentionally engage in the political work that is bound up with power, learning, and technology. Feminist theories can support us in developing or rediscovering more inclusive and equitable tools and spaces. Or as Le Guin ends her essay, "still there are seeds to be gathered, and room in the bag of stars."

Reference List

Alcoff, L. (1991). The problem of speaking for others. *Cultural Critique, 20*, 5–32.

Amiel, T., & Reeves, T.C. (2008). Design-based research and educational technology: Rethinking technology and the research agenda. *Journal of Educational Technology & Society, 11*(4), 29–40.

Anzaldúa, G. (1987). *Borderlands/La Frontera: The new mestiza*. Aunt Lute Books.

Bardzell, S. (2010, April). Feminist HCI: Taking stock and outlining an agenda for design. In *Proceedings of the SIGCHI conference on human factors in computing systems* (pp. 1301–1310). CHI (ACM Conference on Human Factors in Computing Systems).

Bradshaw, A.C. (2018). Reconsidering the instructional design and technology timeline through a lens of social justice. *TechTrends: Linking Research & Practice to Improve Learning, 62*(4), 336–344. https://doi-org.www2.lib.ku.edu/10.1007/s11528-018-0269-6

Carr, A.A., Jonassen, D.H., Litzinger, M.E., & Marra, R.M. (1998). Good ideas to foment educational revolution: The role of systemic change in advancing situated learning, constructivism, and feminist pedagogy. *Educational Technology*, 5–15.

Case, K.A. (Ed.). (2017). *Intersectional pedagogy: Complicating identity and social justice*. Routledge/Taylor & Francis Group.

Costanza-Chock, S. (2018). Design justice: Towards an intersectional feminist framework for design theory and practice. *Proceedings of the Design Research Society*. https://papers.ssrn.com/sol3/papers.cfm?abstract_id=3189696

Crenshaw, K.W. (1990). Mapping the margins: Intersectionality, identity politics, and violence against women of color. *Stanford Law Review, 43*, 1241.

Crenshaw, K.W. (2017). *On intersectionality: Essential writings*. The New Press.

D'Ignazio, C., & Klein, L.F. (2020). *Data feminism*. MIT Press.

Du Bois, W.E.B., & Marable, M. (2015). *Souls of black folk*. Routledge.

Dudek, J., & Heiser, R. (2017). Elements, principles, and critical inquiry for identity-centered design of online environments. *International Journal of E-Learning & Distance Education, 32*(2), 1–18.

Fisher, E. (1979). *Woman's creation: Sexual evolution and the shaping of society*. MacGraw-Hill.

Freire, P. (1970). *Pedagogy of the oppressed*. Seabury.

Gamrat, C. (2020). Inclusive teaching and course design. *EDUCAUSE Review: Transforming Higher Education*. https://er.educause.edu/blogs/2020/2/inclusive-teaching-and-course-design

Haraway, D. (1988). Situated knowledges: The science question in feminism and the privilege of partial perspective. *Feminist Studies, 14*(3), 575–599.

66 Jaclyn Dudek

Hoadley, C., & Cox, C. (2009). What is design knowledge and how do we teach it. *Educating learning technology designers: Guiding and inspiring creators of innovative educational tools*, 19–35.

Hokanson, B. (2020). Design Critique. In J. K. McDonald & R. E. West, *Design for Learning: Principles, Processes, and Praxis*. EdTech Books. Retrieved from https://edtechbooks. org/id/design_critique

hooks, b. (2003). *Teaching community: A pedagogy of hope* (Vol. 36). Psychology Press.

Jen, N. (2018). *Design thinking is Bullsh*t Adobe, 99U conference*. https://99u.adobe.com/ videos/55967/natasha-jen-design-thinking-is-bullshit

Lachheb, A., & Boling, E. (2021). The role of design judgment and reflection in instructional design. In J. K. McDonald & R. E. West, *Design for Learning: Principles, Processes, and Praxis*. EdTech Books. Retrieved from https://edtechbooks.org/id/design_critique

Ladson-Billings, G. (1998). Just what is critical race theory and what's it doing in a nice field like education? *International Journal of Qualitative Studies in Education*, 11(1), 7–24.

Lakoff, G. (2012). Explaining embodied cognition results. *Topics in Cognitive Science*, 4(4), 773–785.

Lather, P. (1988). Feminist perspectives on empowering research methodologies. *Women's Studies International Forum – Pergamon*, 11(6), 569–581.

Le Guin, U. (1986). The carrier bag theory of fiction. *The Ecocriticism Reader: Landmarks in Literary Ecology*, 149–154.

Lyon, G.E. (2022) Where I'm From. http://www.georgeellalyon.com/where.html

Petrina, S. (2004). The politics of curriculum and instructional design/theory/form: Critical problems, projects, units, and modules. *Interchange*, 35(1), 81–126.

Pillow, W.S. (2003). Confession, catharsis, or cure: The use of reflexivity as methodological power in qualitative research. *International Journal of Qualitative Studies in Education*. 16(2), 175–196.

Pink, S. (2008). Mobilising visual ethnography: Making routes, making place and making images. *Forum Qualitative Sozialforschung/Forum: Qualitative Social Research*, 9(3).

Salvo, M.J. (2001). Ethics of engagement: User-centered design and rhetorical methodology. *Technical Communication Quarterly*, 10(3), 273–290.

Sørensen, E. (2009). *The materiality of learning: Technology and knowledge in educational practice*. Cambridge University Press.

St. Pierre, E.A. (1997). Methodology in the fold and the irruption of transgressive data. *International Journal of Qualitative Studies in Education*, 10(2), 175–189.

Stefaniak, J.E., & Baaki, J. (2013). A layered approach to understanding your audience. *Performance Improvement*, 52(6), 5–10.

Stommel, J. (2012). *Hybridity, pt. 2: What is hybrid pedagogy?* Hybrid Pedagogy.

Wong, A. (2022). Disability visibility project. https://disabilityvisibilityproject.com/

A Tale of Two English Teachers

5

Instructional Design Lessons Learned From the Classroom

Erica C. Fleming and Sharon Tjaden-Glass

Erica's Story: Gaining Buy-In

College writing classrooms are unique places. They sit firmly in the realm of general education courses and more often than not my (Erica's) students were completely uninterested in (if not outright hostile toward) the content that I taught. The first time I taught business writing, some students complained that they couldn't understand why my course was necessary. Why was this class required to graduate? Many had received As in their high school English classes, so they believed they already knew how to write.

One student was particularly resistant to both coursework in the class and my feedback on their writing. After receiving a C on their first paper, they came to my office hours to "discuss" (i.e., complain about) their grade. I walked them through my feedback, which was based on the parameters and the evaluative criteria of the assignment, and offered suggestions for improvement for their next paper. However, in an email later in the semester regarding course content, they remarked, "I'm not sure why this matters."

DOI: 10.4324/9781003268413-5

68 Erica C. Fleming and Sharon Tjaden-Glass

That semester, I didn't have a good answer for my student. My background was in English literature, not business or even writing. Much like many college writing instructors, I was a contingent faculty member, working on a by-semester contract. I learned about each class I would teach mere weeks before the semester began (sometimes only days before if I was asked to cover a course that another instructor dropped). I inherited the curriculum from my department and had little time to create lessons and assignments around it, let alone come up with coherent arguments for the legitimacy and importance of my subject matter.

However, over the next few semesters of teaching the course, I developed several persuasive talking points regarding the importance of rhetorical and discipline-specific writing, and particularly how my course taught transferable skills that are relevant in every disciplinary context. This taught me a valuable skill that I later applied to my instructional design work: gaining buy-in. Figuring out how to help faculty see the things that you value (as their instructional designer) as relevant to their work (and, in turn, to gain student buy-in for their course content) has become an integral part of my job. Additionally, the foundational skills taught in the college writing classroom – the rhetorical appeals, reflection, and revision – have all found their way into my work with faculty.

Sharon's Story: Developing Empathy

A few years into teaching English to international students in higher education, I (Sharon) had a student, a young man named Mohammed, who was not only late to every class and never did the homework, but frequently interrupted the class with jokes and displays of his manly bravado. When I asked him to speak to me "in my office" (an open-air desk that I shared with three other adjunct instructors), I was ready to make him run through a gauntlet of blame and shame for not being a better student. That was his problem, wasn't it? But when Mohammed showed up at the meeting, I had a change of heart. For some reason, he looked so much younger outside of the classroom than he did inside of it. Instead, I asked, "What's going on? Are you okay?" With those words, he pinched his tear-filled eyes and looked away. After a moment, he said, "This is the first time that I live without my mother and my sisters."

At that moment, it became clear to me that my students had these complicated, culturally different lives that I knew almost *nothing* about. I could not teach Mohammed without first asking him what he wanted to learn and what was getting in the way of his learning. It was my responsibility to learn about him: to practice cultural humility and be curious about the selves that my students were bringing into our classroom. Not *my* classroom, *our* classroom because we were a community of learners. Now, after 13 years of teaching students from other cultures than my own, I understand that every time that I taught something to my students, I learned twice as much.

What I would learn later through my lived experience as a TESOL (Teaching English to Speakers of Other Languages) professional was that to create effective learning experiences for students, I needed to put them at the center of my decision-making process. To do that, I needed to remember what it was like to be a learner.

In reflecting on my years as a student, I realized that I was constantly trying to figure out how to jump through the hoops that smarter and more experienced people had set up for me. I didn't view classes as learning experiences until graduate school when I was able to apply what I learned in my TESOL pedagogy classes to the intensive English courses I taught to international students as part of my graduate assistantship.

In short, once I made that transition from student jumping through hoops to learner who has a purpose for learning, I more acutely understood the importance of learner-centered pedagogy in my teaching, which then informed my decision-making process as an instructional designer.

Introduction

Our former careers as teachers in higher education impact and influence our current work as course designers and faculty developers daily. This chapter will focus on how our experiences as English faculty members have shaped our instructional design work. Both the content of our courses and our interactions with students have bled into our current work in remarkably positive ways. We believe that the application of these principles could benefit all instructional designers, both within and outside of higher education. Our goal is to introduce you to concepts we both taught and learned in our English courses and then share how you can apply those concepts directly to your instructional design work. Whether you are collaborating with a subject matter expert (typically a faculty member), creating faculty development workshops, or a corporate trainer responsible for both content development and training design, we hope you will try out the techniques that follow each

The College Writing Classroom

At the heart of every college writing lesson is one basic tenet: how can I write to best persuade my audience? Whether students write a proposal, a report, a resume and cover letter, or a definition paper, the underlying goal is to use language to convince an audience that they should listen to what you have to say. This translates into instructional design in unexpected ways. Instructional designers do a really broad range of work, and not all of us design online classes and trainings. While instructional designers work with faculty to design online learning experiences, they also do a variety of other work, such as creating and facilitating corporate trainings and faculty development workshops. Similar to writing classes, instructional designers have to persuade subject matter experts that there are other ways to teach, other tools they could use, and other ways to create excellent learning experiences for their students.

Co-Opting the Art of the Argument

When teaching first-year composition, the starting point is always the audience. Faigley and Selzer's (2012) *Good Reasons with Contemporary Arguments*, a popular first-year composition textbook, offers three audience considerations when starting a written argument:

- You should be "engaged not so much in winning over your audience as in courting your audience's cooperation."
- You should "understand and genuinely respect your listener's or reader's position even if you think the position is ultimately wrong."
- And finally, you should "cultivate a sense of humor and a distinctive voice" (p. 7).

While these lessons focus on helping students become better writers, they can also be valuable in a wide variety of contexts, including convincing students of the importance of this content area (and could have been applied to the student in the story at the beginning of the chapter!).

As an instructional designer (ID), these same three tenets can form a foundation for interactions with faculty members. Subject matter experts do not always understand the benefits and expertise an ID brings to development or revision. Some think that working with an ID means giving up control of their content, while others are resistant to any change to pedagogy, delivery or instructional technology. As such, gaining buy-in from the subject matter expert – which includes helping them understand the role of the ID – is key to effective partnerships.

Whether helping to develop an online course or training, working on a blended course revision, or helping a faculty member use tech tools to encourage more engagement in their course, you can always go back to these three audience considerations. Later – once you gain that precious buy-in – you can share these ideas with faculty to incorporate into their teaching practice. After all, the goals in their classes are similar to those of the instructional designer: they also want buy-in from their students!

Getting Back to the Greeks: Ethos, Logos, and Pathos

One way to gain the highly sought-after buy-in is to make use of the rhetorical appeals of *ethos, logos*, and *pathos*. Students in first-year writing courses are encouraged to appeal to three different aspects of their audience: they needed to convince their audience that they were qualified to write on their topic (*ethos*), appeal to their audience's logic by providing clear, concise arguments backed up by evidence (*logos*), and finally, involve their audience's emotions in some way to get them to care about the topic (*pathos*).

Ethos, or credibility, can be developed in a variety of ways. Sometimes it is enough to include the credentials of the content's author: they may be a leader in their field, have advanced degrees, or have published prolifically on the topic. Sharing these credentials can go a long way to enhance credibility. However, not everyone has this type of inherent credibility, so what do you do then? The answer is both simple and complicated: you have to convince your audience through your arguments that you are *concerned* about the topic and know what is at stake, that you are *well-informed* by borrowing the credibility of others in the field and sharing their work, and that you are *fair* by presenting multiple points of view when necessary.

Logos, or logical appeals, work hand-in-hand with ethos. You want your content to make sense, but logos goes further than that. The best way to develop logos is by citing trusted sources, constructing logical arguments, and presenting content that is clear, concise, and tailored to your audience's current level of understanding.

Pathos is all about how your information is presented to your audience. Research has shown that memory and emotion are closely related; learning that is tied to strong emotions is remembered and retained for longer periods (Tyng et al., 2017). Incorporating emotion into writing is a surefire way to ensure your audience will understand and remember what you have to say. In writing, this looks like using meaningful language, emotional tones, evocative examples, and stories of emotional events to ensure your audience feels a connection to your ideas.

However, all three of these appeals are useless unless you consider the **context** in which the argument will be presented. In Figure 5.1, context is the center focus, surrounded by the *rhetorical triangle*. Centering context forces you to consider the following: who is the audience? What motivated you to engage in this opportunity for change? What do you want your message to accomplish?

The Greek philosopher Aristotle, one of the first philosophers to write about persuasion, originally introduced these concepts in *On Rhetoric: A Theory of Civic Discourse*. He tells us that rhetoric is " the faculty of observing in any given case the available means of persuasion" (Aristotle, 1877, Book 1, Part 2, para. 1). While his points are mainly aimed at philosophers, he makes a compelling argument that the "art of persuasion" applies to every field of study. The field of instructional design is no exception.

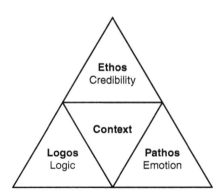

Figure 5.1 The rhetorical appeals

PRACTICE ACTIVITY

Gaining Buy-In and Integrating the Rhetorical Appeals

As an instructional designer, no matter who will be learning from the content you help to develop, your goal is to gain attention, keep attention, and foster knowledge retention. An effective way to do this is to integrate rhetorical appeals into the content of your lessons or training. Instructional designers are well-positioned to do this, as they can often view content from the audiences' perspective.

This process of gaining buy-in also applies to working with subject matter experts, whether they are faculty members or someone who needs to convey information widely in a corporate setting. Because their focus is on disseminating important content and information, subject matter experts place the greatest value on what specific information is included. As an expert in pedagogy, digital tools, and online learning, the instructional designer is poised to focus on taking the subject matter and shaping it into a package that will not be just informative, but also effective and memorable. Sometimes, the same principles that we use to gain buy-in from students and other trainees can be used to gain buy-in from subject matter experts on things like tools, content organization, and delivery strategies.

Questions for gaining buy-in and integrating the rhetorical appeals:

1. **Buy-in**: Does your audience understand why this lesson/training/digital tool/pedagogical strategy is important and relevant? Is this built into the introduction or very beginning of each lesson?
2. **Ethos**: Does your audience believe that you or the person who developed this lesson is an expert in their field, and therefore worthy to be listened to? How can you convey this to them?
3. **Logos**: Have you succeeded in sharing enough information and evidence to ensure your audience will learn and understand?
4. **Pathos**: Do you include stories, examples, and language throughout your lesson or training that will evoke emotion in your audience?

You're Not Done Yet: Reflection and Revision

Once students complete a draft of any writing assignment, there are still multiple steps they need to take before turning in their final piece of writing. Effective first-year writing courses teach students how to appropriately peer review each other's work. This process of both giving and receiving feedback and then making revisions based on that feedback is a valuable life skill and something they would participate in no matter their field. In a professional setting, regardless of context, most people will have someone check their work before they give it to a boss or client. Most importantly, the peer review process forces students to participate in a step in the writing process that they often skip: the process of reflection and revision.

One way to help students fully understand how to reflect upon feedback and revise their work effectively is to encourage them to participate in a version of Gibbs' Reflective Cycle (Gibbs, 1988). Gibbs suggested a six-step process anyone can use to learn from an experience. This process can be applied in a variety of contexts, but in the context of writing, it looks something like Figure 5.2:

1. **Description**: What feedback were you given?
2. **Feelings**: How did you feel when you read the feedback? Did you agree/disagree with what was shared with you?
3. **Evaluation**: What feedback is worth keeping, and what can you dismiss?
4. **Analysis**: How can you best integrate this feedback into your writing?

Figure 5.2 Gibbs' Reflective Learning Cycle

A Tale of Two English Teachers **75**

5. **Conclusion**: After reading this feedback, did you discover any additional areas where your writing could be improved that your reviewer may have missed?

6. **Action plan**: What have you learned about your writing throughout this process that you can apply to future projects?

By asking students to write out the answers to these questions and turn them in with their final assignments, they are pushed to do more than just glance through the feedback and integrate it without thought. It asks them to think critically about what needs to be revised and how they can learn from each feedback experience moving forward. Teaching trainers and faculty members to go through this same process – or going through it yourself after running a training or faculty development session – can be similarly beneficial.

PRACTICE ACTIVITY

Make Reflection and Revision Part of Your Workflow

Whether you are an instructional designer developing training materials and live sessions, online courses for higher education, or faculty development workshops and materials, the reflection and revision process can be beneficial for ensuring ongoing improvement. No course, workshop, or training is perfect the first time it is delivered; any kind of teaching is a process of constant revision. Fortunately, feedback systems are in place for the work we do in most contexts. Whether you have access to student evaluations, faculty evaluations from a friend or colleague, or trainee evaluations, you probably have access to some kind of feedback. Even if you do not, you (or the person delivering the course or training) can create feedback by participating in self-reflection. At the end of any class, workshop, or training session, write down your observations about what worked well and what could be improved from your perspective.

Once you have compiled your feedback, reflect on it using a version of Gibbs' Reflective Cycle (Gibbs, 1988):

1. **Description**: What feedback from stakeholders do you have access to? Have you been keeping track of your observations and self-reflection?

2. **Feelings**: How did you feel when you considered the feedback? Did you agree/disagree with what was shared with you? Does the external feedback align with your thoughts and observations?
3. **Evaluation**: What feedback is worth keeping, and what can you dismiss? Is there a subject matter expert that you can consult with to help make the decision?
4. **Analysis**: How can you best integrate this feedback into your course/workshop/training revisions? Is there content that needs to be added, revised, or removed? Can the learning activities and assessments be improved to meet the needs of the audience?
5. **Conclusion**: Did this feedback reveal any additional areas where your course/workshop/training could be improved that your reviewer(s) may have missed?
6. **Action plan**: What have you learned about your development process throughout this iteration that you can apply to future projects/course developments?

The College ESL Classroom

Ask any TESOL (Teaching English to Speakers of Other Languages) professional for a list of the three most important characteristics of an effective language teacher, and you are sure to hear "culturally sensitive" or "patient" or "flexible." In other words, they are empathetic. Many of them have been cultural outsiders from their experiences traveling, living, and working abroad. The development of intercultural competence requires personal knowledge building, interaction, reflection, and a commitment to continually reexamine one's worldview (Deardorff, 2006).

This ability to imagine the world through a different cultural lens is particularly advantageous for the TESOL professional who transitions to the field of instructional design. Imagining how learners experience an online course, training module, or instructional manual is essential to the work of many instructional designers. Furthermore, growing research and interest in the intersection between eLearning and educational equity uniquely positions TESOL professionals who have firsthand experience in meeting the needs of marginalized learners. In addition to their empathy and intercultural competence, TESOL professionals also possess a unique skill set that often overlaps with the skill set of instructional designers, which can facilitate a career pivot.

Consider the following common tasks of TESOL professionals:

- Perform needs assessments of learners
- Use backward design (Wiggins & McTighe, 2005) to align assessments and classroom activities with learning outcomes
- Collaborate with other teachers
- Use assessment data to modify instruction
- Engage learners in project-based learning to encourage authentic language learning
- Use a blend of implicit and explicit instruction to meet the needs of different learners
- Engage learners in self-assessment and journaling to raise awareness of their learning
- Use multiple means of assessment, both formative and summative

Learning language happens when the content is comprehensible for the learner, and the learner is motivated to learn (Krashen, 1981). As such, effective language teaching stems from a teacher's keen understanding of the needs of their learners and how to create a learning experience that is authentic, context-driven, engaging, and collaborative. Well-designed language instruction directly demonstrates to learners how they will use language in the real world, which increases learner motivation and buy-in, as Erica pointed out earlier in this chapter.

Some of the most engaging language lessons can be designed with authentic texts. For example, beginning language learning lessons can emerge from concrete, external texts, including apartment brochures, grocery store advertisements, and event flyers. These texts can serve as the centerpiece of the lesson by providing real context that leads to discussions about a text's meaning, its purpose, and key vocabulary. In addition, learners can draw upon their real-life experiences with these topics.

With more advanced classes, the learners' texts can become the centerpiece of the lesson. Students can select a piece of writing that they want to improve. Through a combination of individual editing, teacher feedback, and peer review, students can inventory their most common errors, which can then serve as the jumping-off point for subsequent lessons in grammar. For a truly authentic assessment of a student's ability to self-correct their grammatical mistakes, a teacher can provide a copy of the student's unedited, previous draft and ask the student to find and correct their most common errors. Such assessments can be graded with holistic rubrics that focus on the overall comprehensibility of the texts rather than on the number of errors that students correct. In this way, students can be motivated to identify and investigate their patterns of errors – perhaps verb tense consistency, subject-verb agreement, or comma usage – to improve their editing skills.

In addition to being authentic and context-driven, effective language instruction creates space for critical learning during the time that learners spend on a task as well as during reflective learning after the learners have completed the task. Reflective learning, in turn, provides learners the opportunity to solidify their understanding and increase their long-term retention of information.

In this way, the same aspects of curriculum, course, and assessment design that make language learning effective also provide a solid foundation for instructional designers who desire to create meaningful, coherent, and engaging learning experiences for learners and trainees alike.

The Intersection between TESOL and Instructional Design: Learner-Centered Pedagogy

TESOL professionals often have a unique relationship with the content of their field. Unlike teachers in content areas who may adhere to a staunch love for preserving and reciting the content of their discipline (think algebra, chemistry, physics, history), teachers of English as a Second Language tend to be much less attached to what aspects of English they teach in their classroom. Several key reasons for this are that the aspects of English that they teach are highly dependent on the language proficiency of their learners, their students' motivation for learning the language, and the sociopolitical factors that intervene in the language learning process, just to name a few. As such, seasoned TESOL professionals tend to more frequently design instruction and assessments that place learners – rather than content – at the center of the design process.

This familiarity with and devotion to the learner serves transitioning TESOL professionals well as they pivot to instructional design, where learner-centered pedagogy is the beating heart of the field. Instructional designers are called upon for their ability to question and reconsider a course or curriculum from a learner's perspective – and then use their understanding of learning materials, resources, and tools to meet the needs of the learner. In other words, while a learner-centered teacher critically considers *what* the students will learn, the learner-centered instructional designer critically considers *how* the students will learn and then how they will demonstrate their learning (Weimer, 2002).

PRACTICE ACTIVITY

Prioritize the Learner over the Content

Like teaching language, effective instructional design draws upon a keen understanding of the learner, the learning context, and the content. For example, one area to consider is the level of understanding that learners need to demonstrate to show their learning, best exemplified in the different levels of Bloom's revised taxonomy (Anderson & Krathwohl, 2001). As you consider your next instructional design project, grab a stack of sticky notes and reflect on these questions.

1. **Why do learners need to know this content?** List all the reasons on separate sticky notes. These reasons might be related to job requirements, professional development, or personal development. Then, select the top one or two reasons that learners need to know the content. As you move through the project development process, keep these reasons at the forefront of your decision-making.
2. **What attitudes might learners have toward the content that can be acknowledged and addressed in the lesson or training?** For example, employees might be required to learn about uncomfortable and challenging topics like workplace sexual harassment. Designing effective instruction for these topics requires sensitivity and consideration of how the affective domain of learning can influence the cognitive domain of learning.
3. **What motivations for learning the content might the learners bring into the learning experience?** What demotivating factors may pose obstacles for the learners? Record these motivations and obstacles on sticky notes.
4. **What is the content of the project?** For each main topic of the project, write a sticky note that represents the topic. Line up all the sticky notes of the main topics and reconsider the content. Keep in mind your learners' reasons for needing to know the content and their motivations for learning. What content is unnecessary or can be pared down to prioritize other concepts that deserve additional explanation or review? If you are not the subject matter expert

(SME) for the project, consult the SME about the possibility of paring down the content of the project.

5. Finally, **what level of understanding in Bloom's revised taxonomy do learners need to achieve to demonstrate success?** Draw an empty pyramid and label the levels of Bloom's taxonomy: remember, understand, apply, analyze, evaluate, and create. Then, organize the topics of the project's content according to Bloom's taxonomy, with the topics that require the learner to simply remember information at the bottom of the pyramid and topics that require the learner to create something new at the top of the pyramid. Visually separating the topics by the level of understanding that you want learners to reach will help you better identify the range, variety, and balance of assessments that you will need to include in your learning experience design.

Creating Meaningful and Lasting Learning Experiences

Some of the most powerful language instruction stems from project-based learning, in which learners, guided by their curiosity, investigate complex questions in an attempt to better understand a multi-faceted issue to which there are no definitive or correct solutions. In project-based learning, students engage extensively with each other to construct knowledge while their collaborative learning is supported and they are encouraged to direct their inquiries (Condliffe et al., 2017). For example, learners might explore the global issue of plastic pollution in the oceans or possible solutions to the rising deaths due to opioid abuse. Project-based learning empowers learners – guided by their instructors – to select their topic and focus, create a plan for investigating the topic, select a method for assessing their learning, and articulate their motivation for achieving these goals.

In the same way, project-based learning can be a powerful framework for instructional designers in creating meaningful and lasting learning experiences that individually motivate learners and trainees. When learners can demonstrate successful learning simply by reciting a policy or recognizing definitions, instructional materials can be brief and explicit and instructional methods can be didactic. However, when successful learning requires that learners demonstrate higher levels of Bloom's taxonomy, such as analyzing or creating, instructional designers can use project-based learning to inform and structure learning experiences.

PRACTICE ACTIVITY

Align Levels of Understanding with the Level of Assessment

Not all learning can be assessed with multiple-choice and true-false questions, but it's important to remember that *some learning can be assessed this way*. If the goal in designing a learning experience is simply to help learners *remember* some important facts, then a multiple-choice assessment can suffice. However, if learners need to demonstrate that they can *explain, analyze,* or *evaluate,* the learning experience will need a more robust means of assessment for learners to demonstrate their learning. Such learning can better be assessed with rubrics that specify the mastery of learning outcomes that the assessment addresses.

Here are some questions to help you identify which level of understanding a learning experience needs to assess.

1. What content do your learners/trainees/employees need to learn that requires a low level of understanding of Bloom's taxonomy, that is, remembering and understanding?

    Simple and explicit PowerPoint slides, outlines, and infographics can facilitate remembering and understanding. What other types of learning/training materials would be more appropriate and effective for teaching this content?
2. What content do your learners/trainees/employees need to learn that requires a high level of understanding of Bloom's taxonomy, that is, applying, analyzing, evaluating, and creating?

    When learners/trainees/employees need to achieve a deeper level of understanding, they will need more than PowerPoint slides, outlines, and infographics to demonstrate successful learning. Project-based learning, experiential learning, and self-reflection can provide some avenues for learners to analyze, evaluate, and create. What types of problems or issues might your learners/trainees/employees face that require them to demonstrate a higher level of understanding? How might you design a learning

> experience that encourages the learner/trainee/employee to achieve those levels of understanding? What measurable criteria should you include in a rubric that will demonstrate that a learner has met a specific learning outcome?

Conclusion

In this chapter, we have shared our experiences as a means of enriching your practice as an instructional designer. It may even help you better understand colleagues who come from English education or TESOL backgrounds, which can further inform your collaboration with them as well as what they bring into the design process. The main theme of our chapter has been considering the needs of your specific audience. Whether you are gaining buy-in for your content, reviewing audience feedback and reflecting on your work to improve it, or striving to make learner-centered decisions regarding your content, assignments, and delivery, the job of any instructional designer is to ensure that we create effective learning environments for our students or trainees.

Reference List

Anderson, L., & Krathwohl, D. (2001). *A taxonomy for learning, teaching, and assessing*. Addison Wesley Longman.

Aristotle. (1877, 2014). *Rhetoric* (W.R. Roberts, Trans.). The Internet Classics Archive. http://classics.mit.edu/Aristotle/rhetoric.html

Condliffe, B., Quint, J., Visher, M., Bangser, M., Drohojowska, S., Saco, L., & Nelson, E. (2017). *Project-based learning: A literature review*. MDRC. Retrieved April 13, 2022, from www.pblworks.org/sites/default/files/2019-01/MDRC%2BPBL%2BLiterature%2BReview.pdf

Deardorff, D. (2006). Identification and assessment of intercultural competence as a student outcome of internationalization. *Journal of Studies in International Education, 10*(3), 241–266. https://dx.doi.org/10.1177/1028315306287002

Faigley, L., & Selzer, J. (2012). *Good reasons with contemporary arguments* (5th ed.). Pearson Education, Inc.

Gibbs, G. (1988). *Learning by doing: A guide to teaching and learning methods*. Further Education Unit.

Krashen, S. (1981). *Second language acquisition and second language learning*. Pergamon Press.

Tyng, C.M., Amin, H.U., Saad, M.N.M., & Malik, A.S. (2017). The influences of emotion on learning and memory. *Frontiers in Psychology, 8*, 1454. https://doi.org/10.3389/fpsyg.2017.01454

Weimer, M. (2002). *Learner-centered teaching: Five key changes to practice* (1st ed.). Jossey-Bass.

Wiggins, G., & McTighe, J. (2005). *Understanding by design* (2nd ed.). ASCD.

Building Resilient Courses

6

How Crisis Management Can Inform Instructional Design

Chris Gamrat, Edward J. Glantz, and Lisa Lenze

Chris's Story

For five years I worked for the NASA Aerospace Education Services Project as an educational technologist. During that time, I learned a lot about how to make the complex science and engineering at NASA approachable to teachers and students in order to prepare the next generation. I also observed as part of the culture of NASA that the quote from the Apollo 13 mission was true: "Failure is not an option." While not explicit, this was as true for the education programs NASA delivered as it was for a mission to Mars. When I worked with my NASA colleagues to prepare for a new way to bring NASA to the schools, we knew how important it was to be able to provide this service. Much like in Apollo 13, we had plans, back-up plans, and ad hoc solutions based on what we had available at the time. Very often we took advantage of the engineering approach of controlled, observed failures that we can learn from and the importance of iteration in our process to learn from that failure.

From this work, I have always been conscious of what could break in an educational experience I've prepared (course, presentation, etc.) and how we

DOI: 10.4324/9781003268413-6

84 Chris Gamrat, Edward J. Glantz, and Lisa Lenze

might be able to prevent, mitigate, or pivot from this issue. In my prior role as an instructional designer at Penn State's College of Information Sciences & Technology, I learned from my co-author, Edward J. Glantz, and others that there are formalized methodologies for preparedness. In my eight years as an instructional designer, my colleagues and I have consciously and some-times unconsciously continued to develop strategies for crisis prevention in instructional design, which has led to improvements in the experience of the students and faculty – and to tremendous scaling in our course offerings. In this chapter, we translate lessons learned in crisis management into tactics for reducing crises in the design, development, and delivery of online courses, ultimately increasing course resilience.

Introduction

Informed crisis management improves course resilience. In this chapter, we address this theme from the perspective of an instructional design *team*. At our institution, such a team includes an instructional designer (e.g., Chris), an instructor or subject matter expert (e.g., Ed), administration (e.g., Lisa), and a teaching assistant (when relevant and available). Elsewhere, our team has explored the intersection of crisis management and instructional design (Glantz et al., 2021). Here, we document the *process* of how formal crisis management techniques can be used to create more resilient courses. We focus on the element of planned resilience rather than on in-the-moment crises, as typically, when a crisis occurs with a class, it is out of the hands of the instructional designer.

Crises most often occur in either human/social or technology/environ-mental contexts. Human/social disruptions occur with the instructor or students, such as when students catch an illness that cycles through the com-munity and prevents a large number of students from completing class activi-ties. These disruptions prevent instructors and students from engaging with the course as planned. Technology/environmental disruptions occur when an external factor is at play, such as a technology outage or a weather event that prevents the course from running for a period of time. Considering these types of crises, the instructional designer can benefit colleagues by anticipat-ing possible disruptions and finding ways to eliminate or mitigate them.

It is worth noting that this practice is embedded in the ideas behind "continu-ous improvement," such as the Deming Cycle's Plan, Do, Check, Act philosophies (Tague, 2005). In response to global competitors, these strategies were embraced effectively by US manufacturers beginning in the 1970s to improve quality.

Just as manufacturers reacted to changes in quality requirements, we believe instructional designers are changing in conjunction with higher education's movement to online education, remote learning, non-traditional students, varied content, and even dependence on less traditional individuals to develop and deliver course content. How long has it been since you worked leisurely as a facilitator with experienced course authors to develop content delivered face-to-face? Instead, we suspect you have noticed the shift to work exhaustively as an instructional design team member across varied contexts.

In this changing environment, it is even more important to identify what could go wrong early during the design process. This anticipatory approach permits the organized planning and implementation of responses. In doing so, the instructional designer may control hazards as both a defensive tactic and an offensive strategy.

Instructional designers regularly handle crises in courses they are developing, ones that are running, or often both. This chapter provides an overview of a five-step risk assessment process that can be used in the work of instructional designers. These ideas will structure your professional techniques and ensure courses that are more resilient to crisis.

Resilience

We define risk resilience as *the ability to adapt strategies, plans, and decisions in anticipation of potential disruptions.*

The principles of resilience are straightforward and begin with the notion that hazard events may disrupt intended outcomes, such as the successful delivery of course content. The number of these events can be enormous at any given time, so the common response is to accept them, often without even recognizing their existence. In this haphazard wait and see approach, negative events must first manifest to be identified and remediated.

We advocate a more active identification of potential disruptions, followed by their management. For example, the designer could engage the instructional design team in structured analytic techniques to identify potential hazards to the successful design, development, and delivery of course content. Controls for more serious hazards – ranked by likelihood and impact – could be developed in advance to create resilience.

The true benefit of this approach comes from the experience gathered through repetition. Hazard events can be logged to a risk repository that grows each project cycle. Hazards previously deemed less serious can be re-evaluated for change, while other hazards can be added to the repository for evaluation.

Five-Step Methodology

For those new to the practice of resilience, we propose a simple five-step methodology. This methodology is adapted from more exhaustive approaches presented by groups such as the Project Management Institute (PMI), National Institute of Standards and Technology (NIST), and Department of Homeland Security (DHS), for example. These are documented in PMI's PMBOK (7e), NIST Risk Management Framework, and the DHS National Infrastructure Protection Plan (NIPP). Books such as *Measuring and Managing Information Risk: A Factor Analysis of Information Risk (FAIR) Approach* by Freund and Jones (2014) or *Principles of Risk Analysis: Decision Making under Uncertainty* by Charles Yoe (2019) are also available for further information.

The five steps of the methodology are common to any effective risk reduction process and, for example, are implemented by UK's Health and Safety Executive. The organizational benefit to its systems, processes, organization, and people is prompt and effective response to threats and opportunities that may arise.

These steps, listed here and aligned with the Deming Cycle (in parentheses), are discussed further below:

1. Identify hazards (Plan)
2. Assess the hazards (Plan)
3. Control serious hazards (Do)
4. Document findings (Check)
5. Review controls (Act)

Step 1: Identify Hazards

Hazard identification and documentation are both creative and ongoing processes. Four common methods can be used to assist designers in identifying hazards.

- Monitoring literature and news of related disruptions (e.g., an oncoming wave of a highly contagious and long-lasting strain of flu, continuous failure of power grids in unusually warm seasons) can support decision-making about possible risks to technology and pedagogical approaches.

- Ethnographic investigation, including observations and interviews with instructors and students, allows for further understanding of how courses run in different circumstances and helps with the identification of pain points that can be addressed in a course revision.
- Brainstorming with other stakeholders (e.g., administrators, librarians, disability specialists) leads to better understanding of what constitutes a disruption in the course.
- Reviewing historical data (e.g., in student evaluations and faculty peer observation notes) provides additional insight.

Collecting information in these ways supports an instructional designer or design team in considering possible hazards and how they might be addressed.

When conducting this process, you might find that instructional design crises broadly fit into two categories. Some disruptions impact a course development or revision, and some occur while the course is running. When collecting data and brainstorming, it can be valuable to use this approach as an organizer to help in the identification process. While course delivery hazards may appear to be out of an instructional designer's control, in future steps they can still be considered and proactively addressed. Table 6.1 provides a brief example of this exercise.

After utilizing these techniques, designers may have identified many possible hazards that would disrupt the design or delivery of a course. This step is focused on the brainstorming of hazards. If you are conducting this step with a team, make sure to have a space where all participants can contribute.

Table 6.1 Identifying hazards organized by development and delivery of a course

Course Development or Revision	Course Delivery
Course Management System Disruption	Student Missing Class
Schedule Delays	Academic Integrity Violation
Long-term Absence	Teaching Assistant Leaves
Required Technology Approval	Students Do Badly on First Exam
Miscommunications	Inclement Weather Disrupts Class

88 Chris Gamrat, Edward J. Glantz, and Lisa Lenze

Do not limit the power of the pen to a single person as this threatens the full potential of the brainstorming activity. It is likely that at the conclusion of this activity, the group will have generated a substantial list. To prioritize, in the next phase, we will examine the *impact* of the hazards.

PRACTICE ACTIVITY

Identify Hazards

In this section, brainstorm (ideally with others) to consider hazards that would impact your work as an instructional designer. Consider using categories such as "course development" and "course delivery"– or other broad categories that make sense for your context – as a starting point in this phase. Use Table 6.2 for practice.

Table 6.2 Practice table to identify hazards organize into two categories

Hazard Category 1	Hazard Category 2

Step 2: Assess the Hazards

When thinking about how to prioritize your efforts to manage a crisis in instructional design, you might find value in the following risk score formula:

Risk = Likelihood x Impact

Ranking hazard risk scenarios with tools like this and others of your formulation (more on this later) can support strategic decision-making on spending time and money to manage these events. We recommend establishing a rubric (music to the ears of an instructional designer) to determine how to assign point values to likelihood and impact scores assigned to each risk scenario. Using a rubric is also particularly important for inter-rater reliability when scoring with a group or for decision-making. This section will provide a walkthrough with worked examples to calculate risk in course design.

Course Assets

We begin by identifying and ranking the course assets. The process of evaluating and treating risk is best reserved for critical assets, as time and money needed to reduce risk are limited and should be allocated where most beneficial. Learning designers already prioritize critical assets when they elevate extra resources to courses taught across multiple sections or instructors, for example. Courses with large enrolments could also be considered more critical.

For courses deemed critical, the next steps are to (1) identify risk scenarios for each asset, and (2) determine a risk score for each scenario. The risk score (likelihood x impact) is calculated for critical courses to determine higher likelihood, higher probability risk scenarios. For risk scoring to be meaningful, the same rubrics are used to evaluate the likelihood and impact of all risks. Then, (3) treatments to reduce likelihood and impact are recommended for scenarios associated with high risk scores on critical assets.

Risk Scenarios

Identifying risk scenarios or what could go wrong can be done in several ways, benefiting from combining methods. For example, a risk repository of historical problems could be maintained. Another is to conduct a creative structured analytic exercise with a group, such as divergent-convergent analysis or formal brainstorming. Finally, the literature can be reviewed for known or emerging hazards in course development and/or instruction. Examples for the former include instructor-related delays in development and, for the latter, a course management system (CMS) failure.

Now we're going to assess the hazards by assigning likelihood and impact scores to each.

90 Chris Gamrat, Edward J. Glantz, and Lisa Lenze

Table 6.3 Example listing of possible course disruptions in the development or delivery of a course

Risk Scenario
Student Missing Class
Minor Project Delay
Course Management System Disruption
Schedule Delays
Long-term Absence
Required Technology Approval
Miscommunications
CMS Outage
Academic Integrity Concerns
Teaching Assistant Availability
Students Do Badly on First Exam
Inclement Weather Disrupts Class

Likelihood Scoring

Like in Table 6.4, a likelihood scorecard or rubric is created to assign values to the likelihood of each risk scenario (see worked examples in Table 6.5). You can use linear or other value range increases but clearly explain each value in percentage probability and description. In other words, this scoring associates a value to the probability of a given event and by identifying the likelihood, the designer is identifying what might prevent a smooth development and delivery of the course. Note that the likelihood description terms used here are adapted from former Central Intelligence Agency (CIA) analyst Sherman Kent (Arnett, 2015), who espoused the adoption and use of clear, standardized "words of estimative probability" when describing likelihood.

Impact Scoring

Similarly, an impact scorecard is created to assign values to the impact of each risk scenario.

Below is an example impact scorecard in learning design risk scenarios that can impact either development or delivery.

Building Resilient Courses **91**

Table 6.4 Example of a **likelihood scorecard** created to evaluate risk
scenarios

Likelihood Score	Probability %	Likelihood Description
5	87% and up	Almost certain
4	60% to < 87%	Probable
3	40% to < 60%	Even chance
2	12% to < 40%	Probably not
1	< 12%	Almost certainly not

Table 6.5 **Impact scorecard** created The Pennsylvania State University
designers to evaluate development and delivery risk scenarios

Impact Score	Learning Design Impact Description: Development or Delivery
25	Instruction or CMS disrupted for more than eight hours for more than 300 students • Or – Effectively unusable project outcomes
20	Instruction or CMS disrupted for more than eight hours for 200 to 300 students • Or – Failure to meet key milestones
15	Instruction or CMS disrupted for more than four hours for 100 to 200 students • Or – Moderate delay affects key stakeholders
10	Instruction or CMS disrupted for two to four hours for less than 100 students • Or – Slight slippage of key deadlines
5	Instruction or CMS disrupted for less than two hours for less than 100 students • Or – Slight reduction in quality and scope

92 Chris Gamrat, Edward J. Glantz, and Lisa Lenze

Again, you have the freedom to use linear or other value range increases but should clearly describe each value. Impact descriptions in the impact scorecard should be broad enough to score the entire range of risk scenarios. In this case, impact scoring for development and delivery scenarios are included.

When working with a team, you might also want to examine impact using your formulas. In the Penn State College of Information Sciences and Technology's Office of Learning Design, when we have staffing changes for instructional designers and need to redistribute the courses assigned, we evaluate courses on a degree of complexity. Complexity includes factors such as the following:

- Number of times the course is offered per year
- Number of students per section
- Courses with labs or resources that require setup or configuration
- If the course has a current or upcoming revision

While this calculation might not be perfect, it gives the design team perspective into the dimensions of work (and potential impact) and allows for better communication across the team and leadership (if needed).

PRACTICE ACTIVITY

Impact Scorecard

In Table 6.6, create a scorecard or rubric to assign a weight for evaluating risk scenarios.

Table 6.6 Practice **impact scorecard** for evaluating risk scenarios by ascribing a value to the scenario's impact

Score	Learning Design Impact Description: Development or Delivery
25	
20	
15	
10	
5	

Risk Score Table

The risk scenarios are listed in a table, and the likelihood and impact scores are entered. Finally, the risk score is calculated by multiplying the scores together. Typically, the final risk scenarios are listed from the highest score at the top. Table 6.7 provides some example risk scenarios and possible scores that a team might assign.

When determining likelihood and impact, we recommend documenting impact with colleagues, if possible, and using a rubric to support your decision-making. This provides a degree of inter-rater reliability when quantifying these variables.

By conducting this process, we have determined that students missing class is the highest risk of the brainstormed list as it is very likely, especially with large enrolment courses, and the impact is toward the middle of the spectrum as it could affect student group work and mean the loss of important discussions and other activities in class. The impact score would increase as the number of classes missed increased.

Table 6.7 Example of **risk score matrix** with a score calculated for each risk scenario by multiplying likelihood and impact scores, ranked from highest at top

Risk Scenario	Likelihood Score	Impact Score	Risk Score
Student Missing Class	5	25	125
Minor Project Delay	4	25	100
Course Management System Disruption	5	20	100
Schedule Delays	5	15	75
Long-term Absence	3	15	45
Required Technology Approval	2	10	20
Miscommunications	2	10	20
CMS Outage	2	10	20
Academic Integrity Violation	1	5	5
Teaching Assistant Leaves	1	5	5
Students Do Badly on First Exam	1	5	5
Inclement Weather Disrupts Class	1	5	5

94 Chris Gamrat, Edward J. Glantz, and Lisa Lenze

PRACTICE ACTIVITY

Document Hazard Impact

In Table 6.8, take the identified hazards and apply the formula Risk = Likelihood x Impact to determine the highest risk hazards. This will help you to prioritize your efforts when trying to manage potential crises.

Table 6.8 Practice table of risk scenarios ranked with calculated risk value by multiplying likelihood and impact scores

Risk Scenario	Likelihood Score	Impact Score	Risk Value (Likelihood x Impact)

Step 3: Control Serious Hazards

Additional controls can be planned for more critical hazards (i.e., those of greater likelihood and/or impact). Risks are ideally controlled in advance by reducing likelihood. A proactive consideration for controlling instructional design hazards is establishing common shared best practices. To

Building Resilient Courses **95**

this effect, we advocate for a standard course template that reduces hazards in multiple ways:

1. Students are less likely to struggle to find things in a course when there is standardization to navigation and course structure.
2. Faculty new to teaching have a place to start that is a collection of scrutinized instructional design considerations.
3. The template iterates each term based on the instructional designer's experiences, including lived crises and lessons learned.

A long-term strategy for controlling hazards in instructional design is to strive for continuous improvement. As time progresses, designers return to the brainstorming and impact exercises to identify efforts needed to improve the process.

If little can be done to influence likelihood, efforts to lower impact are developed. Some crises can emerge through the unique needs of students (ranging from accessibility needs, an individualized accommodation, to group work, a multi-faceted group dynamic). For accessibility accommodations, some efforts can be integrated into the course development process by advocating awareness of making accessible content such as HTML, presentation slides, or videos. Given the staffing in an instructional design unit, focus on tasks such as captioning video or providing detailed descriptions for images might be shifted to others. Also, while it is ideal to have all of this work completed before the course runs for the first time, resource limitations might require that this is an effort that is again prioritized based on need and impact.

Another course crisis that could be mitigated with design considerations is in the area of group work. For a variety of reasons, not all groups are successful. First, discuss with your instructor the purpose of the group work. Using a critical lens, examine if the group effort is needed as an objective of the course or if it detracts (e.g., in a course where students must learn the basics and group work allows less able students to hide among more capable peers). In situations where group work is warranted, the development of a group contract can establish expectations for group dynamics and at least initial ideas on steps toward resolution of conflict. If a group becomes dysfunctional, a resilient course design would have options for what the instructor and students might do if the dysfunction cannot be resolved.

In the hazard impact example in Table 6.3, the highest risk identified is students missing class. Since this is something that very likely cannot be avoided

96　Chris Gamrat, Edward J. Glantz, and Lisa Lenze

Table 6.9 Example hazard controls across course elements

Course Component	Control Strategy
Syllabus	Discuss policies for late assignments, attendance, and in-class participation
Group Work	Implement group contracts that help students to identify how to proceed if one of their group members is not able to contribute
In-Class Activities	Develop activities or alternatives that can be done outside of class
Lectures	Develop a strategy for recording lectures or capturing specific elements of the course that would help missing students get caught up

and the instructional designer is not directly involved in the running of the course, all of the designed controls should be developed with the instructor and built into the course upfront. These student absence controls can be categorized by the various components of the course, as shown in Table 6.9. This exercise demonstrates breaking the hazard into smaller chunks and implementing a series of controls to reduce the impact.

PRACTICE ACTIVITY

Create Hazard Controls

After weighing risks, identify elements of the course and corresponding controls that can be used to minimize the hazards in Table 6.10.

Table 6.10 Practice hazard control identification across course elements

Course Component	Control Strategy

Step 4: Document Findings (Check)

Even the best-laid plans need review and modification, and thus we make time to document our resilience plan progress. Here we monitor whether we have appropriately identified serious hazards, as well as the contingency plans. We add those to our risk repository as we develop responses to lower impact and/or likelihood if new hazards arise. We may also document recognized hazards no longer deemed a significant threat, thereby conserving scarce labor and material resources.

This documentation of findings is referred to as the check stage in the Deming Cycle, and in risk resilience, it serves an even more critical role. Contingency plans need to be evaluated for problems they might create. In creating contingencies, we change the process and should repeat hazard identification to recognize potential issues arising from the contingency. In other words, by solving one issue, we may inadvertently create another.

For example, in response to the 9/11 attacks, airplane cockpit doors were hardened to prevent outside threats. Unfortunately, this created a new threat from within for foreign airlines without a two-person rule, resulting in several tragedies. This might have been recognized had hazard identification been repeated.

In higher education, consider the instructor who wishes to improve academic rigor with high-stakes assignments devoid of student feedback. While the addition of high-stakes assignments may resolve the absence of rigor, a new problem of jeopardized learning effectiveness may emerge from the lack of feedback. Thus, contingencies should be evaluated for potential problems. We suggest making use of this process periodically, and to revisit the brainstorming process when considering the implications of changes made by the instructional design team.

Step 5: Review Controls with Stakeholders

Effective risk management requires *risk communication* among stakeholders. For instructional design projects, stakeholders can include faculty, teaching assistants, multimedia specialists, librarians, technical support, and department/college leadership.

Effective risk communication with stakeholders includes establishing, reviewing, and confirming hazard controls among multiple levels of

Figure 6.1 Layers of authority to establish hazard controls

authority. Figure 6.1 depicts three common levels of decision authority for establishing and implementing hazard controls. At a basic level, some controls are set by the instructional designer and can be implemented right away as the designer has the authority to make certain decisions about how they work. The second layer, unit authority, requires an established agreement on a process, guideline, or policy for the instructional design unit. Finally, at the department/college level, controls can become a complex workflow of decision points, approvals, and consequences depending on whether course design work is completed on time and to the level of quality expected. As there are many people involved and their roles are varied, controls may need to be collaboratively developed to support the creation of high-quality learning experiences.

In addition to decision authority, trigger events and redundancies to lower impact may need to be identified and communicated, resulting in effective member responses. Trigger events can include situations where if development milestones are not met, the result is an escalation to leadership to evaluate the situation. Instructional design teams can also lower the likelihood or impact of hazards through regular share out meetings and by assigning backup designers for each course/project to manage questions or other issues that come up if the primary instructional designer isn't available. Furthermore, flowcharting can also document the process to show the points where all stakeholders become involved and the decisions and responsibility each person yields. This kind of documentation minimizes questions of who is responsible and when crisis mitigation strategies might be triggered along the process. For example, Figure 6.2. demonstrates a decision point in which the instructional design team has established a date/time to evaluate if the course is ready to be offered or in the following term. At Penn State's College of Information Sciences and Technology we refer to this as a go/no go for launch date (another lesson learned from the culture and vocabulary of NASA).

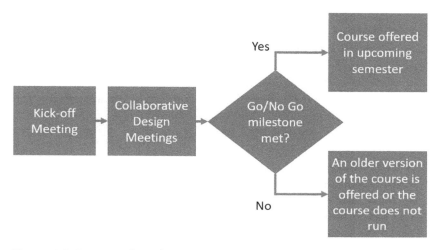

Figure 6.2 Decision flow diagram evaluating if a course development has met expectations on an established timeline with decisions to offer the course if the deadline is met or not

Review/Update Risk Assessment

The five-step method we overviewed has limited utility if the activity is only done once. Resilience depends on planned and continuous improvement. Risk assessment is a critical element of continuous improvement. Adjustments can be implemented in the instructional design process as part of a regularly scheduled revision and should also be implemented after a crisis event. These events offer a learning opportunity to examine what happened and improve the design. We believe it is worth investing the time to make more resilient courses.

Our experience with reviewing a master's level course in Cybersecurity Analytics (course number IST 820) provides a good example of routine risk assessment as part of continuous improvement. During our annual program review, we investigated the learning outcomes associated with the final project in IST 820, a prominent course in an online master's degree in Cybersecurity Analytics and Operations. We discovered that students met the outcomes but not without questions and unnecessary struggles along the way.

In our attempts to understand the difficulties, we assembled a team of stakeholders: instructional designer, instructors teaching the course, the assessment administrator, and the director of master's programs. We considered students' readiness for the tasks assigned in the final project, discussed the assignment task, and reviewed the rubric. Upon closer inspection, we noticed that the directions for completing the assignment were not aligned with the rubric. This design imperfection led to many student questions about completing the assignment and what to include in the written paper.

Out of our continuous improvement efforts, IST 820 emerged with a better final assignment description and accompanying rubric. When we assess the course again, we hope that students spend more time working on the paper and less time determining what to do, thereby strengthening the resilience of the learning assessments.

Practical Takeaways

We hope you've found ideas from the field crisis management that you can leverage into your practices from this chapter. Here, we offer practical takeaways that designers are uniquely positioned to promote among administrators and faculty partners.

For the administrator: Well-designed course development (or course revision) contracts assist in mitigating one of the most prevalent risks in the design process: missed deadlines. Contracts should include targeted delivery expectations, along with milestones toward achievement. Learning designers are well-positioned to assist administrators in writing such contracts, given designers' familiarity with appropriate timelines for producing deliverables.

Similarly, the learning designer can advise the contracting unit to consider including design expectations in *teaching* contracts. These could include, for example, expectations to teach the first offering of the course and thereby provide an opportunity for final tweaking.

To bolster course resilience, contracts for faculty who will teach recently developed courses could include pay-it-forward expectations. For example, instructors could be contracted to embellish on rubrics that are minimally serviceable, contribute quiz items to build more robust question banks, or gather student feedback on particular course elements. As a member of the instructional design team, the learning designer would provide valuable insights into each course's needs.

For the instructor: Course authors are responsible for contributing as active members of the instructional design team during course design, development, and delivery. Each of these stages contains potential pitfalls that should be recognized in advance, along with planning for contingencies.

For example, schedule conflicts may prevent the author from making necessary progress. In this case, the learning designer could share progress information during periodic contracting unit review sessions. The designer serves a critical role in creating awareness of factors negatively impacting the design and development of the course.

Designers are also able to influence resilience in course *delivery*. For example, online courses often include unique pacing requirements. Weekend days constitute most of the work time during which non-traditional students complete assignments. Similarly, many faculty – especially adjunct faculty – budget course time for the same days. Learning designers can advise course authors to space assignments accordingly to reflect the realities of student and faculty schedules.

Additional course *delivery* concerns include individual and community crisis events. Many instructors (especially new instructors) are not familiar with crisis support resources available through their institutions and professional organizations. These resources may include emergency protocols for dealing with distressed students, planning and assessment tools when moving from one mode of delivery to another, shared instructional design networks for trouble-shooting instructional technology issues, centralized teaching support units to address teaching or learning concerns, and campus emergency alert systems for campus-wide announcements (in residential programs). Learning designers – often the first person an instructor will contact when issues arise during the semester – can equip instructors with resources for crisis events. Creating and updating a resource file before each semester allows designers to respond when instructors inquire.

Conclusion

Walk a mile (or two) in the shoes of the instructor. Whether you can teach at your university or shadow an instructor from a semester's start to finish, the experience will offer a greater understanding of the crises that arise as a course is running. This understanding will improve your ability to anticipate *both* design-based and delivery-based crises in your work as an instructional designer.

Reference List

Arnett, G. (2015). How probable is "probable"? *The Guardian.* www.theguardian.com/news/datablog/2015/aug/14/how-probable-is-probable

Freund, J., & Jones, J. (2014). *Measuring and managing information risk: A factor analysis of information risk (FAIR) approach* (1st ed., 408 p.). Butterworth-Heinemann. ISBN-13: 978–0124202313

Glantz, E., Gamrat, C., & Lenze, L. (2021, November). *Plan and pivot: Flexing instruction through crisis management techniques* [Conference presentation]. 2019 Association for Educational Communications and Technology Annual Conference.

Tague, N.R. (2005). *The quality toolbox* (2nd ed., 584 p.). ASQ Quality Press. ISBN: 978-0-87389-639-9

Yoe, C. (2019). *Principles of risk analysis: Decision making under uncertainty* (2nd ed., 816 p.). CRC Press. ISBN-13: 978–1138478206

Always on Stage

7

Acting and Improv Skills for Creating More Collaborative Design Dynamics

Penny Ralston-Berg and Megan Kohler

Megan's Story

For as long as I can remember I wanted to be an actor. As a child, my elementary school took us to see a live performance of Charles Dickens *A Christmas Carol* at a local theater. I was entranced by the entire experience, entering through the heavy glass paneled doors which opened into the dimly lit lobby and walking up the grand staircase with burgundy colored carpeting. Grasping onto the cold metal handrail wrapped in multiple layers of blue paint depicting years of use from many other students and patrons of the theater. The squeaking sound made by the springs of the velvet covered seats when unfolded. When the lights dimmed and the performance began, I was completely transported. I knew at that moment I wanted to be an actor.

After graduating high school, I delayed going to college to pursue my dream of acting. Within a few months, I found myself auditioning with a

DOI: 10.4324/9781003268413-7

touring company. In the world of theater audition pieces are often only a few minutes in length. The reason being that a casting director usually knows within the first 30 seconds of a performance whether or not you can play the part they are casting for. At the end of my audition, the director offered me the job. I was cast as the female lead in a three-person version of *A Christmas Carol*. The very play that inspired me as a child, now became the entry point into a world that would change me forever.

When I first started acting, I believed performing the lines of the play flawlessly was the most critical aspect of acting, in other words, being excellent at your job. In working with the touring company, I encountered many seasoned professionals who recognized my passion for acting and taught me that being a strong actor encompassed much more than a single person's performance. They taught me that a show isn't comprised of a group of individuals on stage reciting lines. An impactful performance could only be achieved if everyone in the troupe worked together with open communication and generous collaboration. Building relationships led to trust, and that trust allowed us to stay safe and creatively explore new ideas when working together.

Although I eventually left acting to pursue instructional design, the skills I developed as an actor were invaluable treasures that I carried into my practice as a designer. I truly believe the skills taught to actors have the capacity for us to become better peers and to create more positive working environments for everyone. In doing so, we can support each other, pursue more innovative ideas, and create better learning experiences for students. Most importantly, we can collaborate in ways that allow everyone's strengths to shine so that each team member can have their moment in the spotlight.

Penny's Story

I've been a lifelong fan of television and film. Many years ago, I quit my job as a video store clerk to return to college to study television production.

> Definition note: To watch movies at home prior to broadband Internet and streaming services, people needed to go to a physical video store to rent video tapes or DVDs to take home and watch. Late fees and rewinding charges were a thing.

In addition to my formal studies, I also had the opportunity to work at the student television club to produce gameshows and comedy sketch shows. I learned how to collaboratively write and produce shows with input from other writers, producers, directors, and actors. I also learned about improvisation and how what happens outside the script can add value to the final show. I appreciated the actors' interpretation and additions to my scripts – adding jokes or using the props in a creative way.

After graduating and while working as an assistant television producer, I began volunteering as a light and sound technician at the local community theater. I learned to stay alert and be ready for anything, such as an actor skipping four pages of dialogue, the line to end a scene and kill the lights being slightly modified, or an actor improvising completely new lines during the live performance. Following the script exactly as it is printed is not always the path to success. Improvisation and trust allow for mistakes and changes to be accepted and used to continue the show. Being open to ideas, present in the moment, observant, and actively listening helped me react quickly and positively to a variety of challenges.

The same concepts can apply to working relationships. Even within a design or project team, we're still in a performance together. As a designer, I work with a variety of subject matter experts (SMEs) and other professionals to design and develop online learning. Within such a team, it's not uncommon for people to disagree or suggest what appear to be disparate ideas. By accepting ideas, feedback, or suggestions from others as gifts and responding in a positive way, we can keep the project moving forward possibly in a new, better direction. Even a statement from a SME such as, "I don't like your idea. It won't work," is a gift that can spark further conversation. The statement can be shocking, but by thinking quickly and reacting in a positive way by asking, "Can you tell me more about what you don't like about it?" keeps the conversation moving forward. Although improvisation can sometimes be uncomfortable, it can also lead to better designs.

A Theatrical Influence

Actors (and those who support them) must be prepared to engage with others, build trust, and use a variety of skills to respond quickly to different situations. This helps actors maintain their character and keep the scene moving forward in the event something unexpected happens. In the world of live theater, it's possible for a prop to break, a costume to become torn, a cue to be missed, a line to be forgotten, a cell phone to ring, and any other number of events which can easily distract the actors and possibly even the audience during a performance. But "the show must go on."

In these unexpected scenarios actors need to provide information and ask questions to keep scenes moving forward. In a live stage performance, an actor cannot break character and let a fellow actor know they just skipped over a piece of dialogue or placed a prop in the wrong location. The actors must maintain character and continue to live in the world of the play. Actors must think quickly in the moment, stay positive, and collaborate with fellow actors to get things back on track.

Instructional designers are not actors but can borrow from the world of acting and improvisation to add tools to their designers' toolbox. Designers will likely experience the unexpected. Just as in live theater, things can go wrong or not as the designer planned.

- A subject matter expert (SME) may not know what designers do or the value they add, and you may find yourself defending your value in the first meeting.
- A SME may not like an approved design, and you need to explain your design rationale to persuade them or ask questions to get information needed to revise the design.
- The project team members, parameters, budget, or deadlines may change, and adjustments need to be made.
- The SME may have a design in mind prior to project kick-off which doesn't meet the desired outcomes, and you need to keep the conversation moving forward in a positive way.
- The SME may have competing priorities and doesn't have time to spend collaborating with you, and you must adjust your usual process.
- The SME may provide some content pieces and believe their contribution to the project is complete.
- A SME may have heard stories from a colleague about a negative experience working with a designer and project that experience onto you.

When confronted with the unexpected, designers have the choice to react negatively and "kill the scene," saying or doing something that ends the conversation or react positively in a way that keeps the conversation moving forward. All of these scenarios require skills in building collaboration and trust, communicating effectively, and creatively solving problems in the moment.

Collaboration

During a play, everyone relies on one another to put on a successful performance. Everyone is valued regardless of their role or responsibility within the performance. When things don't go as planned on stage, actors engage in improv to ask questions or share information to keep the scene moving forward. Through receiving and sharing information from fellow actors, challenges are overcome, and the performance continues. They must view everything they receive from other actors as a gift to be received and quickly incorporated into their work on stage. Positive or negative, they must receive that gift and work with one another to keep the momentum of the scene going. To reject that gift means the end of the scene. Tina Fey describes how live performances can be derailed by denying or disagreeing during a scene (Google Talks, 2011). This negative response leaves fellow performers with nothing to work with or build on to keep things moving forward. It kills the scene for the actors and the audience. Accepting or agreeing to what is given is key.

In design, there are many circumstances in which we are handed both mindsets and materials that are positive and negative. Our job is to accept each gift and let go of our preconceived expectations to keep the project moving forward. To give up or to quickly reject what our collaborators offer will negatively impact the relationship and may ultimately result in being removed from the project or possibly even the cancellation of the project. Collaboration is at the heart of any effective design project. Individuals with different types of expertise work together toward a common goal. If collaboration isn't present, especially between the designer and SME, the overall product will be lower quality and as a result, the learner will have a poor experience (Aleckson & Ralston-Berg, 2011).

Strategies for Enhancing Collaboration

Allow Everyone to Have a Voice

How do you become a better collaborator? First, start by finding ways to give everyone on the team a voice. For the first few rehearsals of a new show, all the actors attend in order to learn about the work and to ensure everyone understands the director's vision. Thereby allowing everyone to connect with one another, to feel seen, and to be heard. For design projects, you can have a kick-off meeting in which everyone (SMEs, other designers, multimedia specialists, programmers, librarians, and other experts) all have a say in identifying the goals, risks, parameters, and direction of the work (Kohler & Ralston-Berg, 2020). Getting everyone involved from the start of the project allows all perspectives to be included in the brainstorming. Explain the purpose and rules of collaborative brainstorming meetings from the beginning – that all team members are valued, the meeting is a safe space to share ideas, and initially, all ideas will be accepted and not judged as they are shared.

Make Others Look Good

How would you feel if in every meeting you attended, your colleagues did and said things that made you look good? Those meetings would likely be much more enjoyable for you, wouldn't they? That's the point. In working toward making your peers look good, you present yourself as a positive, supportive, and collaborative colleague. This skill goes against everything anyone in the business world has ever been taught, but it's definitely one that should be included into our design toolkits. As the saying goes "A rising tide lifts all boats." Aim to bring positivity to the dynamic and raise others up whenever you can. You might be surprised when others begin doing the same and in turn contribute to a more enjoyable workplace culture.

Maintain Composure

The above advice also comes with an important consideration. There will always be individuals who will take the gift of your kindness then give you negativity in return. The reality is that you can't control the words and actions of others. What you do and how you handle yourself in those situations says far more about you than the other person ever could. Which means you should demonstrate your integrity, professionalism, and maturity regardless of the actions of others. By maintaining your composure and acting professionally in all circumstances, you will establish a solid reputation for yourself. Designers are more effective and valuable when SMEs and other collaborators see them as positive, approachable, and helpful.

PRACTICE ACTIVITY

Enhancing your Collaboration Skills

Actors engage in a number of games or other activities to help develop the skills necessary for becoming strong collaborators. The following activities are taken from the world of theater and can be used to develop or enhance your collaboration and communication skills. Play these games with friends or designer colleagues to practice how to give and receive information, encourage everyone to contribute, and build on what others propose in a positive way.

Gifts

This game helps designers practice receiving and reacting to unexpected or confusing information in a positive way. Working in pairs or small groups, practice giving and receiving gifts while making positive comments.

1. This game begins with selecting a gift giver. Without speaking, the giver selects another player and mimes giving them a gift, being sure to express characteristics of the gift (size, weight, shape, etc.).
2. The recipient mimes opening the gift, saying what it is, and thanks the giver.
3. The recipient then becomes the next gift giver and selects a new player to receive the next gift.
4. Repeat for 5 minutes. Continue to give and receive gifts within your group or pair.

Collaborative Cartoon

This game helps designers practice appreciating and expanding upon the contributions of others.

1. Provide a background image or an empty comic strip either on paper or digitally.

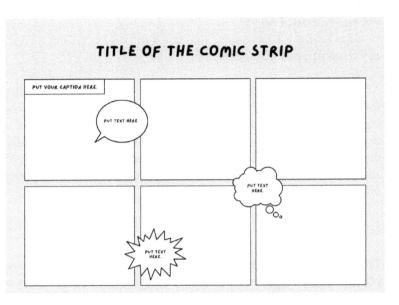

Figure 7.1 Blank six-panel grid comic strip, Marketplace Designers, Canva.com

2. Ask each player to add items so that a collective scene or comic is created with everyone contributing at least one item. The game can also be played in rounds, with each player taking turns contributing something in each round.

Yes, And . . .

This is a game about accepting a gift (of information) from another person, then adding to the story to keep things moving forward. Two players engage in conversation using "Yes, and. . ." to drive the conversation forward.

1. In pairs, one player begins a story.
2. The other person replies "Yes, and . . ." and then makes a statement to keep the story moving forward, being sure to provide

Figure 7.2 "Yes, and . . ." conversation bubbles

enough details and information for the other player to work with in their next response.
3. Continue back and forth. Each time a person speaks, the other player says, "Yes, and . . ." followed by a new statement.
4. Play for 5–10 exchanges.

Scenario: Brainstorming Ideas

This scenario illustrates how these collaboration skills may be incorporated into a working meeting with SMEs and teams. The facilitator demonstrates skills in receiving information and staying positive, uses a structured activity to ensure everyone makes a contribution, and encourages forward thinking by supporting the ideas of others.

> A project manager calls together a project team – a lead designer, two SMEs, two additional designers, a multimedia specialist, a videographer, and a programmer. The team's goal is to create an immersive, multimedia rich language learning experience. The desired outcome of the meeting is to brainstorm what such an experience might look like and document the requirements so that the lead designer and project manager

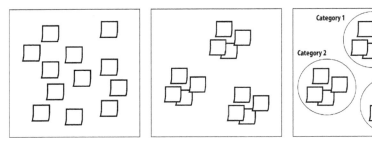

Figure 7.3 Idea sorting with sticky notes

have enough information to scope out an initial prototype. The team is a mix of introverts and extroverts; colleagues who work together often and strangers who have never met; and those with less experience with online learning working alongside seasoned experts with many years of experience. The SMEs and most experienced team members are the most vocal, comfortably sharing the many possibilities they have been considering. Others listen carefully as ideas are presented and immediately judge if the idea should be included in the project or not. Some members of the team sit quietly and don't interject their ideas into the conversation. All team members were included based on their unique areas of expertise and all have good ideas to contribute, but not all are participating in the meeting. How can the lead designer who is serving as the meeting facilitator be sure everyone's ideas are heard and valued?

Breakdown: In this scenario, a few team members are dominating the meeting, and the facilitator needs to purposefully include everyone at the meeting. The facilitator also needs to model the expected behavior by staying positive, encouraging others to share ideas, and working to move the conversation forward.

Strategy: As some team members are not sharing ideas verbally, give everyone an opportunity to share ideas in a non-verbal way. One method is the KJ Method in which each team member works on their own to add individual ideas to slips of paper, cards, or sticky notes (or digital notes in the case of virtual teams). The notes are then shared with all, sorted into clusters, categorized, and discussed (Iba et al., 2017). This method encourages all team members to contribute ideas and reserves judgment and discussion until later in the process.

During the conversation to sort the ideas, be sure to model positive conversation by supporting ideas of others, asking questions or making statements to encourage others to elaborate on their thoughts about categories, and keep the conversation moving forward.

Trust

In theater, there is an expectation that everyone wants the performance to be successful and each individual is willing to do their part to ensure that even if something unexpected might happen, an actor knows the other members of the troupe will offer support to help work through the circumstance. If a single person chooses not to follow through, it can negatively impact the other actors and ultimately the performance. This sense of trust becomes the foundation by which the team can build relationships, take ownership of their responsibilities, and most importantly recognize the value of their contribution to the larger group.

The expectation is the same on design teams. The belief that the team will support one another during the design, development, and delivery of a high-quality course/product is the gold standard. Unfortunately, far too often breakdowns in communications and the relationships lead to lasting conflict. Our egos become bruised and personal agendas cloud the goals of the team, which detract from producing quality work. Trust is extremely fragile, and once it is broken, it takes a significant amount of work to restore it. With this in mind, it becomes much easier and more efficient to work toward maintaining trust than to try and restore it after it's been lost. Without trust, a team can't survive. In any type of performance, it is understood that everyone will fulfill their commitment to the team. This type of trust becomes the tie that binds the team together.

Strategies for Building and Maintaining Trust

Developing your Character (Persona)

In order for an actor to portray a character, they need to have a comprehensive understanding of who that character is. An actor might think about the character and try to answer deeply personal questions such as "How does this person like their eggs?" "How do they take their coffee?" and "What's their favorite book?" As a reader you might be wondering why this is important. Well, the answer is simple. Because it's not until we truly know someone at the deepest levels that we can understand why they make the choices they do. Since a play follows various characters through a series of circumstances and choices they have to make, this helps an actor understand why a character makes the choices that they do. The same is true for us as designers and even more so as human beings. Who are we as designers? What aspects of teaching and learning are we most passionate about? What are our goals for a meeting? Understanding who we are as designers helps us better understand how we can have a greater impact in our profession. Spend some time reflecting on the projects you've worked on and try to answer a few questions such as "What did I most enjoy about this project?", "What do I value within this work?", and "What drives me to continue doing this work?" Interestingly enough, you can use the answers to these questions when you formulate your personal elevator pitch.

Vulnerability

To join a group of actors in creating a world of play, one needs to be willing to share a creative part of themselves. This can be extremely intimidating because you're sharing your thoughts and your talents, thereby opening yourself up to the judgment of others. This vulnerability can only occur in a safe environment, where you can share with others who will be gentle and compassionate with your work. This type of environment differs significantly from the everyday workplace environment. Rarely are we afforded the opportunity to be our authentic selves. We are frequently required to share our work with others without the safety and care that is experienced in the world of acting. In the workplace, our creations are often criticized by SMEs and supervisors, our ideas stolen by thoughtless co-workers, and our creativity buried by financial restrictions. Yet we cease to give up. Every day is a fresh start and design, much like how theater is an art form. Despite the potential for criticism, vulnerability is an important aspect of both gaining and maintaining trust. It requires us to open our hearts and trust that others will be gentle.

PRACTICE ACTIVITY

Deepening Trust Among Collaborators

Actors engage in a number of games or other activities to help develop the skills necessary for building trust. The following activities can be used to create a persona or show vulnerability while supporting others. Play these games alone, with friends, or with designer colleagues to practice being reflective and showing vulnerability and support while working with others.

One-Minute Persona

Set a timer for one minute. Create a persona for yourself. What are your hopes, fears, goals, and values? Set another one-minute timer and consider how other team members perceive you. Create a persona describing you from their point of view.

Five Questions

Using your persona as a starting point, quickly compose five questions others might ask to learn more about your goals, values, and project vision.

Infomercial

Present a late-night infomercial selling your services and value to your team member or SME. Why should they work with you? If possible, include artifacts or demonstrations that demonstrate your expertise.

ABC Story

Players tell a story one line at a time. Each line must begin with the next letter of the alphabet. The audience chooses the starting letter. Support the other players by giving enough information for them to work with and build on to keep the story moving forward. Also support other players who may lose track of the current letter.

Figure 7.4 ABC conversation bubbles

Scenario: The Unknown Designer

This scenario illustrates how trust between the design and SME or other collaborators may be absent at the start of a project or course development.

> The SME has no experience working with a designer and doesn't understand why they've been assigned to work with one. They don't trust the designer to be as committed to the success of the project as they are. The SME doubts the designer will add any value to the project team.
>
> **Breakdown:** The SME likely is not being purposefully difficult or malicious in any way. In this case, the SME simply doesn't know anything about the designer's experience and is unaware of the value they may add to the project. They have nothing on which to base their trust.
>
> **Strategy:** Think of your course/project launch as the performance. Accept what the SME offers, respond positively, and work toward building trust gradually. Find ways to establish common goals. Demonstrate your value and expertise through examples of past work, research on best practices, and the rationale behind your design suggestions. Reassure the SME that you are on the same side and share a common goal of creating a successful project/course.

Communication

Communication is essential for not only a successful performance, but the safety for every actor in the troupe. When choreographing a fight scene, a dance, or simply the movements on stage, it's important for actors to disclose when they feel uncomfortable with a movement or placement. Not doing so could result in a serious injury, either for them or one of their fellow actors. To a company of performers, their limitations, expectations, and concerns are recognized and respected. It is through the tactful, honest, and non-judgmental way in which actors communicate their observations and ideas that the company of actors is able to thrive. When two people have different perspectives on how a challenge should be addressed, there is an open discussion with both parties genuinely dedicated to the support of their counterpart while adequately having their own personal needs addressed.

It's important for designers to communicate in ways that present them as helpful and approachable, especially when building collaborative relationships and trust with SMEs. Designers are consultants. In the design of a product or course, a designer and SME may approach the project in different ways and see differing solutions to meet desired outcomes. If the designer pushes back and considers only their own point of view, opposition can grow. But if the designer works to consider the SME's point of view and works to express ideas openly, supportively, and clearly, then both work toward a common goal.

Strategies for Better Communication

Seeing the Other Perspective

The following illustration demonstrates what resistance is like in our conversations. When we try to express our viewpoints and try to win a discussion or an argument, we are pushing in opposite directions. However, the reality is that when one person pushes harder against the other person, the person on the receiving end matches the level of pressure exerted on them. If we truly want to have impactful communication, we need to learn to let go of the need and desire to control, turn into the other person's point of view, and help them meet their goals.

Active Listening

Active listening is more than just simply paying attention. Active listeners must prepare to listen by being open and accepting of others' ideas, observe verbal and non-verbal cues while listening, and provide feedback or ask questions to show engagement in the conversation. During a live performance, a cue only happens once, and it happens very quickly. If you're not paying attention to your fellow actors as they recite their lines, the entire performance can be

Communication in Opposition   Communication Toward a Common Goal

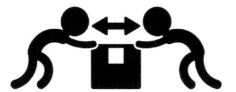 

Figure 7.5 Two ways of communicating: in opposition and toward a common goal

thrown off. This is why it is critically important for an actor to listen carefully. A single moment can have a very negative impact if not handled correctly. The same is true of our design collaborations. If a designer isn't listening carefully, they could miss an important detail which could cause the cost of the project to increase, the timeline to be impacted, and ultimately result in a very unhappy SME. Fortunately, there are ways in which you can practice active listening to increase your ability to listen with intentionality and purpose. Like all other strategies we've shared here, this skill can be developed by engaging in practice.

> ### PRACTICE THIS
>
> *Growing Your Communication Skills*
>
> Actors engage in a number of games or other activities to help develop the skills necessary for becoming better listeners. The following activities can be used to generate collaborative stories, actively listen, ask supportive questions, and empathize with others. Play these games alone, with friends, or with designer colleagues to practice understanding another's perspective and active listening.
>
> ### One Word Story
>
> Each person in the group takes a turn adding one word to the story. Players must listen and add words that keep the story moving forward.
>
>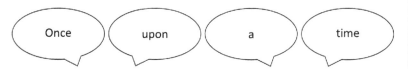
>
> Figure 7.6 One-word story conversation bubbles
>
> ### Questions Only
>
> Carry on a conversation using only questions – no statements. Players must listen carefully to ask questions relevant to the story while

providing enough information for other players to build on and move the conversation forward.

Figure 7.7 Questions-only conversation bubbles

Role-Play

Two players take the role of the SME and designer who are working on a project together. The players or audience can provide a challenge. Players must interact and quickly assess the situation to make appropriate comments or ask questions. This is a good way to practice staying positive during what may be a difficult conversation. Debrief after the conversation. What strategies were effective?

Figure 7.8 Role-playing conversation bubbles

Scenario: The Missing SME

This scenario illustrates how a designer can use empathy to improve a working relationship with a SME.

> A SME and designer have been assigned to work together, but the SME has canceled meetings and not provided any project materials to the

designer. The designer labels the SME as "difficult" and decides to spend more time working with other more collaborative SMEs.

Breakdown: The easiest thing to do is nothing – to move on to other projects and spend less time with this inactive or seemingly disinterested SME. However, designers have a commitment to learners to try to collaborate with SMEs to produce the best possible products/courses within the working constraints and timeline.

Strategy: Empathize with the SME. Do they have other responsibilities that impact the time they have available to work with the designer? What can the designer do to help the SME be more responsive? Schedule a meeting with the SME to discuss the project and other things that impact the SME's availability. Actively listen and ask questions to fully understand the SME's situation. Use that information to create a plan to move forward with work.

Creative Problem-Solving Skills

In acting, things do not always go as planned on stage. An actor may skip a page of dialogue crucial to the plot of the play. Without it, the audience will not understand the meaning behind the big reveal at the close of the play. Nothing will make sense. The other actors on stage quickly notice the error and begin to ask questions and alter their own lines to deliver the crucial pieces of information to the audience. By collaborating, communicating, and trusting one another, they are able to think quickly in the moment to creatively solve the problem and save the show.

In design, problems may not be as obvious as a dropped line or misplaced prop. The design, performance may take the form of team meetings, personal interactions with SMEs, or team efforts to launch a product/course. Challenges can arise at any time during the design, development, or delivery processes. Often challenges must be addressed in the moment with the designer quickly thinking of potential solutions while maintaining composure.

Strategies for Creative Problem-Solving

Using Everything

The Sherlock Holmes series by Sir Arthur Conan Doyle shares the adventures of one of fiction's most creative problem-solvers. Many actors have played this

Always on Stage **121**

role and many audience members have marveled at the journey this beloved character has taken them on. He narrowly escapes harrowing scenarios using only his intellect. However, that's not the entire story. Sherlock has the ability to observe the most minute details and make connections between clues like no other protagonist. In other words, he uses everything at his disposal to solve crimes: his skills of observation, his vast knowledge set, resources left behind or supplied by his enemies, his closest friend Watson who becomes a sounding board for ideas. He uses everything that is available to him in order to creatively problem-solve. As designers, we have to do the same thing. SMEs may leave behind clues within documents they send to us, or we need to observe small details about the graphics that a colleague creates for a course. The vast knowledge a designer acquires by working with a wide variety of professionals, increases our ability to creatively problem-solve, just like Sherlock Holmes.

Don't Rush to Solutions

If a designer is too attached to the notion of how things *should* happen, they may be caught off guard and unable to respond in a way that helps keep conversations or projects moving forward. However, if a designer acts too quickly, reacting without considering underlying issues or what may be the root of the problem, their proposed solution may not be appropriate. Designers need to clearly define and understand problems before reacting to them. To effectively and quickly problem-solve, designers must be able to notice all aspects of a problem, let go of their preconceived expectations of what *should* happen, and use all the information and resources available to find a solution (Poynton, 2014).

PRACTICE THIS

Cultivating Creative Problem-Solving

The following activities can be used to think creatively outside the obvious and react positively to what may be distracting information. Play these games with friends or designer colleagues to practice using information shared with you and thinking beyond obvious solutions or answers.

Everyday Object

Select an everyday object such as a cup, hat, or table. Ask all team members to add potential uses of the item to a shared document. Team members do not communicate about or delete items from the list. They only add their thoughts about how the object might be used.

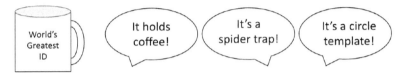

Figure 7.9 Everyday object conversation bubbles

Five Things

Play in pairs or in small groups. Select a person and ask them to name five things in the category of your choice. They must answer as quickly as possible. After answering, they select another person and a new category to repeat the process.

Interrupted Story

Play in pairs. One player begins telling a story. The listener spontaneously provides a word and that must be immediately incorporated into the story. Storytellers need to accept everything that is given to them and not reject the new idea. Switch roles and repeat.

Figure 7.10 Interrupted story conversation bubbles

Scenario: Learner Complaints

This case illustrates how a designer and SME can work together to solve an ambiguous, ill-structured challenge.

Unexpectedly, a lead course designer receives an email from the SME which informs the designer that learners currently taking an online course are complaining and not happy with the course design. The SME reports that technology in the course is not working, there is too much work, and the entire course needs to be redesigned prior to its next offering. They describe the situation as a disaster and want to make plans to revise the course right away. The designer had spent a considerable amount of time collaborating with the SME on the design of the course and was surprised by the request.

The designer and SME have a common goal to make the best possible online course within their timeline. To help identify specific problems that need to be addressed, the designer asks the SME for specific learner comments. The SME provides information that two students are receiving an overwhelming number of notifications and messages from the course. Upon investigation and after asking the students for more information, it was determined that they had unintentionally subscribed to all the course discussions and were getting a notification whenever any students posted or replied to the course discussions – all of them. Tech support was able to work with the students to unsubscribe from the discussions and also to adjust their course notifications to a more manageable amount. The designer also talked to the SME about some other student comments complaining about the amount of coursework students were required to complete each week. In reviewing the course and module learning objectives and estimating the amount of time required to complete work for the previous modules, the designer and SME agreed that there was an appropriate amount of work for a 400-level course.

Breakdown: Complaints can sometimes be ambiguous and undefined. Defining the actual problem leads to possible solutions and actionable items. As a designer, are you able to ask good questions and determine what the actual problems are?

Strategy: Accept the SME's comments and acknowledge their concern. Practice asking questions to draw more information from the

SME and further define the problem. Perhaps specific learner comments are available.

Conclusion

Actors are prepared. They learn lines and cues and practice prior to performance. But they must also be prepared to react to unplanned events in a positive way to provide information to their fellow performers and keep scenes moving forward. Likewise, instructional designers must react positively in the moment to keep their collaborative relationships moving forward. At first, designers may not find this easy to achieve. Reacting in the moment may feel uncomfortable or disorienting when events veer from the expected process.

The practice activities provided in this chapter can be performed with friends or design colleagues to practice your acting and improvisational skills in a safe environment. Through practice, you can become more comfortable with ambiguity and surprises and learn to keep your composure and quickly adapt when the unexpected happens. You may also find yourself being more open and going into meetings with a less rigid preconceived expectation of how things should go. In consulting relationships, trust may not be present at first, but can be built over time. But you can trust yourself and focus on what you can control.

Theater has the ability to significantly influence the field of instructional design through enhancing our collaboration, trust, communication, and creative problem-solving skills, each of which can dramatically change the way we interact and build relationships with our institutional colleagues. During a play, everyone has a critical role, regardless of whether they are the lead actor or an understudy. They are part of a team, and they must rely on one another to put on a successful performance. If something goes wrong during a live show, everyone must pull together to work through it. This happens to be a fundamental truth of design teams as well.

Reference List

Aleckson, J., & Ralston-Berg, P. (2011). *MindMeld: Micro-collaboration between eLearning designers and instructor experts*. Atwood Publishing.

Google Talks. (2011, April 21). *Bossypants: Tina fey* [Video]. YouTube. www.youtube.com/watch?v=M8Mkufm3ncc

Iba, T., Yoshikawa, A., & Munakata, K. (2017, October 24). *Philosophy and methodology of clustering in pattern mining: KJ method invented by a Japanese Anthropologist – Kawakita, Jiro.* HILLSIDE Proceedings of the Conference on Pattern Languages of Programs, 11 p.

Kohler, M., & Ralston-Berg, P. (2020, November). *Collaborative content design: An ideal vision for Course creation.* Presentation at the OLC Accelerate Conference. Online.

Poynton, R. (2014). *Do improvise: Less push. More pause. Better results. A new approach to work (and life).* The Do Book Company.

Designing Therapeutic Landscapes for Learners

What a Critical Health Geography Approach Can Add to the Field of Instructional Design

Michelle Deborah Majeed

Michelle's Story

It is difficult to imagine a time in my life when conversations around health have not been present. Both my parents were nurses, so while I was growing up, dinner table conversations could range from the mundane day-to-day realities of healthcare delivery to critical debates on health equity and access to care. As a second-generation immigrant, I also understood from an early age that understandings of health and health-seeking behaviors were socially and culturally constructed as many in my family grew up in a country where medical pluralism, "an environment in which there is more than one medical tradition" (Crandon, 1986, p. 473) existed and the community continued to use a form of plant-based medicine, colloquially termed *bush medicine* (Tyrell et al., 2020). These familial experiences were reinforced when I began to work in the mental health sector while completing my undergraduate degree and witnessed the barriers that many members of ethno-cultural communities

DOI: 10.4324/9781003268413-8

experienced when seeking culturally appropriate care for themselves or loved ones. This led to a focus on migrant health for my graduate research and an engagement with health geography as it allowed me to explore how the migration experience, the literal movement from one place to another, and the connections between places impacted understandings of health and health-seeking behaviors.

It is equally challenging to remember a time when I didn't see myself teaching in higher education one day. In the years between my degrees, I continued to work in the mental health sector and was drawn to anti-stigma and community development work, essentially, teaching in the community for a diversity of learners (e.g., high school students, police departments, ethno-cultural communities). The impetus for returning to university to complete a doctoral degree was to teach at the post-secondary level. After several years of working as a TA, I hit a wall professionally and needed support to advance my teaching practice. That led me to the Teaching Assistant's Training Program (TATP) at the University of Toronto, which is a peer-to-peer program for graduate-student learners who support each other in their teaching. During my consultations with colleagues in the program, I realized that I wanted to do teaching support work. I spent the next three years as a trainer and then coordinator in the program and then moved forward with a career in educational development, working as an instructional consultant at several colleges and universities in Canada and the US. At the same time, I continued to work as a faculty member teaching in geography, social sciences, and health studies departments with more and more of my teaching occurring online. I applied this hands-on experience to my consultations with faculty and programs, making the shift to online learning and subtly began to shift the focus of my work to creating online learning environments. When the pandemic started in March 2020, my worlds collided; my academic research on geographies of health and well-being became even more important and relevant to the work I was undertaking as an instructional designer.

The chapter will begin with an overview of my current research project that draws the health geography concept of therapeutic landscapes into conversation with pedagogical research. I will then share how place, a key concept in geographic thought, has been conceptualized in the discipline and how health geographers have used it to engage with concepts of health and well-being. With these definitions in hand, the chapter will then highlight how geographic thinking supports a critical engagement with issues related to how learners access and experience virtual and physical learning environments and considerations for hybrid learning. Throughout the chapter, I will

128 Michelle Deborah Majeed

provide questions and prompts that can support the consideration of place in your instructional design practice.

Incorporating Therapeutic Landscapes into Instructional Design

This section will outline my current research project informed by my teaching practice and experiences during the pandemic, my work as a health geographer, and definitions of place and well-being used in the discipline.

Let's start with a little history and theory. The 1990s were a significant period for the development of the subdiscipline of health geography since it engaged with additional theoretical developments in geography, a focus on the conceptualization of place, and a broader holistic understanding of health (each of these elements will be addressed later in the chapter). In 1992, Wil Gesler, introduced the concept of *therapeutic landscapes* to geographers to support a new research agenda that would take up new theoretical developments in the social sciences. Defined by Gesler (1996) as where the "physical and built environments, social conditions, and human perceptions combine to produce an atmosphere which is conducive to healing" (p. 96), the concept of therapeutic landscapes has been a highly influential concept in health geography and is understood as a fundamental feature of health geography's broader engagement with health and place (Andrews, 2017b).

Over the years, the concept has grown beyond Gesler's initial interest in the healing properties of sites of pilgrimage, such as Lourdes, France or Bath, England (Gesler, 1996, 1998), to a metaphor that describes "a particular type of well-being experience associated with healing, recovery, restoration, and place" (Andrews, 2017b, p. 59), and health geographers have explored how maintenance of health and well-being are tied to these sites, not only through their physical characteristics but also as a result of the interactions and networks that are embedded in them (Cattell et al., 2008; Chakrabarti, 2010; Conradson, 2005; Williams, 2002). By engaging with the concept of well-being drawn from the World Health Organization's definition of health, Doughty (2018) writes that "the therapeutic landscape approach is particularly well suited to explore the multitude of spaces where well-being, as a complex emergent process, may be realised and promoted" (p. 348). As such, the concept can be a powerful tool for understanding the lived experiences of learners during the pandemic and the relationships between health and learning and between in-person and virtual spaces during these unprecedented times.

In March 2020, due to public health measures in place to stop the spread of the newly detected COVID-19 pathogen, many colleges and universities in North America shut down their campuses and shifted learning online. I was teaching an introduction to health geography course in the Spring/Summer 2020 term. At the time of the course, Ontario, Canada was still in lockdown with public schools, daycares, community centers, and even outdoor parks and trails closed. College and university campuses as well as student residences were also closed, and most learners had returned home (within Canada or internationally). Despite all of this, post-secondary institutions continued to offer courses, and learners continued to enroll and attend classes online, either synchronously or asynchronously. Halfway through the term, I gave a class on the concept of therapeutic landscapes. I also opened up an ungraded discussion board asking learners the questions listed below.

Sample Online Discussion Board Questions – Spring 2020

1. Prior to COVID-19 lockdowns, what constituted a therapeutic landscape for you (e.g., your bedroom, local park, rec center, hiking trail)?
2. Do you still have access to your therapeutic landscape?
   - If you do, does it still feel therapeutic, why or why not (e.g., if your home was your therapeutic landscape, three months stuck inside might change your feeling towards it)?
   - If you don't have access anymore, have you been able to find another place that supports your overall health and well-being? What alternative have you used (e.g., maybe you don't have access to the gym so now you use workout videos at home)?

I was surprised at how many of my learners responded and with the stories they shared. It was clear that the pandemic had impacted their therapeutic landscapes and that they wanted to share those experiences. It was also clear that learners were re-making their therapeutic landscapes or finding alternatives, illustrating a level of metacognition and awareness of the characteristics of places they found health-promoting and an application of this knowledge.

Considering the responses I received, I felt it was important to document and further understand the experiences of learners and the strategies they employed to support their well-being. Thus, this research seeks to understand how the therapeutic landscapes of undergraduate learners have been impacted

130 Michelle Deborah Majeed

by the shift to remote learning in their post-secondary studies because of the COVID-19 pandemic. Furthermore, this work recognizes that learners' access to therapeutic landscapes have been further impacted by public health measures and restrictions placed on their communities. As such, this research project explores how the intersectional aspects of learners' identities, social positionality, and lived experiences impact their ability to (re)create spaces that support their health and well-being during a global pandemic. The time, energy, and metacognitive aspects of this labor on the part of learners needs further consideration in terms of the rapid shift to remote learning and the impending shift back to in-person learning to assess the impacts on their health and well-being.

While remote learning disseminates academic education through online spaces, the learners themselves occupy physical spaces that must be adapted to the new learning demand and these spaces have their own material limitations and barriers. This research project seeks to understand how learners attempt to shape their environments to support their well-being while continuing their education during a pandemic.

For example, with the closure of universities, learners have lost access to campus spaces that supported their health and well-being (e.g., green and nature spaces on and around campus, quiet study spaces, activities hosted by learner support services). Additionally, learners have also lost access to spaces they characterize as sites that support productive academic work (e.g., libraries, cafes, other campus spaces). Due to campus closures, these productive sites have often shifted off-campus to locations that were previously characterized by learners as therapeutic spaces (e.g., bedroom, kitchen table, home). This has forced learners to seek out resources and develop strategies to support the division of work and rest in these locations and/or seek out new locations that can provide similar productive or therapeutic value. Thus, learners are engaging in the construction of therapeutic landscapes in relation to the spaces they need to complete the productive work associated with their identity as learners.

While the COVID epidemic has intensified the shift to remote learning, online learning is unlikely to disappear when the pandemic is resolved, and we will likely see a shift to a more permanent online and hybrid approaches to teaching and learning. As such, guidance on future opportunities for accessing therapeutic landscapes and holistic health resources should be explored and examined to reconsider how post-secondary institutions can support learners on and off campus as well as physically and virtually. Based on the research outlined above, I have added a few practices to my teaching to support the discussion and creation of therapeutic landscapes for learners. Below is a list of practices and prompts to consider when approaching this topic from an instructional design perspective.

PRACTICE ACTIVITY

Therapeutic Landscapes Questions and Prompts

The following practices and prompts will help you to bring therapeutic landscape considerations into your practice or your work with instructors or subject matter experts (SME):

1. Similar to the discussion board activity shared in this section, an ice-breaker activity at the beginning of the course can be used to help learners share the spaces they consider therapeutic and identify the characteristics of them. To support this community-building activity, be prepared to share a little about the places you find health-promoting and why.

2. Once learners share their experiences, also ask them for any strategies or resources they use to support the maintenance of their therapeutic landscapes. Consider creating a shared discussion board or editable page or document where learners can add their thoughts and share with peers.

3. Based on what learners identify in the conversations above, consider how to incorporate some of the considerations and strategies into the course development. For example, create a check-in time at the beginning of each class so students can share something about their week. You can start these conversations with a story from your week to model the type of sharing that is appropriate. After a few weeks, you can support community building practices by following up with students about stories they have shared previously.

4. Consider how you can add in therapeutic elements (e.g., an outside classroom walk and talks, photos, sounds). These could coincide with relevant term dates. For example, I have incorporated mindfulness sessions, with the support of one of my teaching assistants, into the first class of the term, around midterms, and in the last week of the course. The first class introduced the idea at the beginning of the term to learners, and the second two were linked to high-stress times of the term. You can do something similar by using a mindfulness app that provides short sessions.

5. Be mindful that not all students will find the substance of these sessions helpful, but they will appreciate time being given to support their well-being!

The remainder of the chapter will outline how instructional designers can take up aspects of health geography's larger conceptualization of place and well-being beyond therapeutic landscapes and into their own design practice. Each of the following sections will highlight one health geography concept, its relevance to instructional design, and provide some prompts and practices to support the incorporation of these concepts into the design process.

What is Place?

It is difficult to talk about place without mentioning space, since they are understood as the two foundational concepts in geography. It would also be ahistoric to talk about how place has been taken up in health geography without understanding the debates and divisions that have developed between the sub-disciplines of medical and health geography.

Health geography is a relatively new subdiscipline, born out of the more established field of medical geography. Almost three decades ago, Kearns (1993) called for a post-medical geography that would take up a place-sensitive approach to the study of health by moving away from medical geography's focus on geometric conceptualization of space and seeking further engagement with new theoretical developments in geography and social sciences more broadly (Kearns & Collins, 2010). Prior to Kearns' prompting, medical geography, owing to what has been termed as the *quantitative revolution* in geography and other social sciences was characterized by its positivist and quantitative approaches to research and a focus on spatial analysis and disease ecology (Andrews, 2017a). In medical geography, space is the focus of analysis with place characterized as static, mappable locations that support spatial analysis (Andrews, 2017a; Kearns & Collins, 2010). For example, it is through the concept of place that space can be identified, divided, and compared (e.g., to support the analysis of the allocation of health services and resources in a particular location). Furthermore, the relationship between places is also available for calculating and mapping patterns (e.g., spread of disease from one place to another) (Andrews, 2017a).

Kearns' call created a lively debate in the field (Mayer & Meade, 1994; Dorn & Laws, 1994) that resulted in the conceptualization of place becoming central to the field of health geography (Kearns & Collins, 2010). As Andrews (2017a) writes, "understanding has developed in geography that health and health care are deeply affected by places and the ways in which places are reacted to, felt and represented" (p. 44). While place has become the focus of inquiry for health geographers, they have approached the conceptualization of the relationship between health and place in multiple ways. Two understandings that are relevant to this chapter and instructional design are place as a social construction and place as relational.

Place as Social Construction

As Andrews (2017a) writes, "'people make places' and 'places make people'" (p. 44). Moving beyond the conceptualization of place as location that is found in medical geography, health geographers turned to the work of geographers who applied humanist and phenomenological approaches to understanding and conceptualizing place (Tuan, 1979; Eyles, 1985). According to Gesler and Kearns (2002), humanist approaches aim to "understand personal experiences and feeling and how people attach meaning to their surroundings" (p. 23). Experiences of a place are understood to be informed by the social, political, and economic structures that exist and the individual's positionality within them. It also recognizes that this sense of place may not be the same for everyone, with some having positive experiences, while others can experience the same place negatively. As such, health geographers have focused on how places are socially constructed and experienced, ultimately arguing that place matters to health and health care (Kearns & Collins, 2010).

Considerations for Instructional Design

Taking up a conceptualization of place as socially constructed, I would argue that as instructional designers we are the people that make places. Furthermore, as the people with this power, we need to consider how places make people in assessing how the learning spaces we create impact learners and how to engage them in the co-creation of spaces of learning. Furthermore, by changing the location of a learning space, either online or in-person, we also alter how learners will engage with and experience them. Additionally,

134 Michelle Deborah Majeed

the sense of place within the learning environment will be different among users because of their own positionality inside and outside these places.

PRACTICE ACTIVITY

Geographic Questions and Prompts

The following prompts will help you to bring geographic considerations into your practice or your work with instructors or subject matter experts (SME):

1. Take a few minutes to reflect on your previous experiences as a learner and choose a positive or negative one. This can be a formal (classroom) or informal (learning a new skill from a family member) experience, or an in-person or online learning experience. What values or characteristics do you feel support your learning in these spaces? What values or characteristics may create barriers to your learning? If you are working with an instructor or SME, ask them to also complete this activity.
2. Review the list you and/or your collaborator(s) have created. Consider how your own learning experiences influence how you design a course or the elements you consider necessary for a successful learning experience in the course you are designing. For example, maybe you or your collaborator(s) have indicated you learn better in a community with peers. Has this filtered into the course by developing online discussion boards or in-person group work activities?
3. Once you have reflected on how you create a sense of place in your learning environments, turn your attention to the learners that will occupy them. Consider making your values and considerations explicit for learners, perhaps through a value statement for the course.
4. Now consider what processes or activities can be developed to provide learners the ability to co-create a sense of place within the learning environment (e.g., reconfiguring the seats in the classroom or moving the learning out of the classroom to nature spaces, expectations on how learners and instructors can move

through a learning space, community developed guidelines, peer feedback, online discussion boards, and how learners can engage in this process (e.g., class discussion, shared document, anonymous survey, personalizing their online avatars in online learning spaces). For example, create a draft list of classroom guidelines that includes values and practices you believe are important, share them with the class, and then ask learners to suggest revisions and/or additional guidelines that will also support their learning.

Place as Relational

While humanist and phenomenological approaches have allowed for nuanced and rich understandings of places, one of the critiques of these approaches in health geography is that places are often characterized as static, discrete, and hold intrinsic properties (Andrews, 2017a). Drawing on the larger relational turn in the social sciences, some geographers have taken up a relational approach that centers place in its analysis. As Andrews (2017a) explains,

> Simply put, it [relational thinking] implies a twist in how place is theorised, evoking an image of places emerging not only 'in situ,' but also through their connections within networks of 'translocal interactions.' In other words, places are highly related to, and produced by, many other places at multiple scales.
>
> (p. 46)

Thus, a relational approach to research highlights the fluid boundaries of places, change in the content of places, and mobility across places (Cummins et al., 2007).

For health geographers, taking up a relational approach has allowed us to reconsider the relational connections that inform understandings of health and health experiences. For example, in my research on the health experiences of Guyanese immigrants in North America, I argue that their health experiences in the countries of settlement continue to be informed by their previous experiences in the country of origin. My research found that the historical use of traditional bush medicine provided a resilience response to inaccessible biomedical healthcare in Guyana. However, the continued use of bush medicine in the countries of settlement is not a result of barriers to healthcare. Instead, continued use constitutes a health practice that is tied to historical use, perceived efficacy of treatments, and participants' perceptions of Guyana as a positive and healthy place (Majeed, 2021). As such, the countries of origin and settlement must be placed into conversation with each other in order to understand the plurality of experiences and health understandings that are simultaneously engaged with in each location.

Considerations for Instructional Design

To take up a relational understanding of place in instructional design, I would argue that we must recognize that learning environments are not hermetically sealed, and a learner's experience in a teaching space will be informed by the space in of itself as well as in relation to other spaces that are concurrently and previously experienced. Thus, learners are drawing from a plurality of experiences and places, historic and contemporary, when engaging in the learning space. Furthermore, considering the rapid shift to online learning, we must recognize that there is always a body attached. While learners are learning in online spaces, they are also living material lives that impact their perceptions and their ability to engage virtually. Additionally, as instructional designers, we need to consider how understandings of relational place can support learner engagement inside and outside the classroom (virtual or in-person) and across various locations.

PRACTICE ACTIVITY

Relational Geography Questions and Prompts

The following prompts will help you to bring geographic considerations into your practice or your work with instructors or subject matter experts (SME):

1. Take a few minutes to reflect on the mode(s) of delivery of the course that is being developed (e.g., in-person, online, hybrid). What are some of the assumptions made about these spaces and engagement with students in them? How are these assumptions

informing the design process? For example, if a course is being offered online, is the expectation that learners do not need to engage in-person with their instructor, colleagues, or the physical space of campus?

2. Now consider what processes or activities can be developed to engage both online and material spaces during the learning process. For example, a flipped classroom model would allow learners to engage with course content (e.g., readings, presentations, multimedia resources) prior to entering a physical learning space that will then inform their work in that space (e.g., in-person discussions, group work). Another option is that students in an online class are asked to engage with their local physical environments to complete an activity (e.g., for an urban geography course, they are asked to walk around their neighborhood to document the relationship between the built and natural environments) and then share it online with their colleagues.

3. Additionally, are there opportunities for learners to interact with each other across different learning environments? For example, if there are online and in-person sections of the same course, are there opportunities built into the course for learners to interact with each other?

Understandings of Health and Well-being in Health Geography

The other significant difference between medical and health geography is how health has been defined and measured. Medical geography, as its title suggests, has at its core a Western, biomedical definition of health focused on disease pathology and measurements of health (e.g., levels of mortality, morbidity) and the provision and use of health services across different locations (Kearns & Collins, 2010). While health geographers also address issues related to disease and health care in their work, they have extended their understandings of health beyond the biomedical focus on the absence of disease to a more holistic approach that considers the whole person and their communities. One of the grounding definitions for health in the subdiscipline comes from the World Health Organization's (WHO)

138 Michelle Deborah Majeed

constitution that defines health as, "a state of complete physical, mental, and social well-being and not merely the absence of disease and infirmity" (WHO, 1948, p. 100). With the discipline's focus on how experiences of places impact the health of individuals and communities, the WHO's definition provides health geography the breadth to investigate subjective experiences of place across a multitude of factors and characteristics and generates policies that can support inclusive, positive health strategies that considers local realities.

Over the years, health geographers have continued to deepen their theoretical engagement with the concept of well-being, which finds its roots in the WHO's definition. At its most fundamental level, well-being can be defined as "being-well," and assumes that one is healthy, happy, and generally feeling good about your quality of life (Andrews, 2017b). However, as Kearns and Andrews (2010) note "being as a state of existence can only be achieved through place" (p. 63). Fleuret and Atkinson (2007) argue that the concept of well-being provides health geographers the opportunity for further research because the concept is taken up differently across multiple social and spatial locations. However, as Kearns and Collins (2010) have cautioned, "a critical and place-sensitive perspective must be maintained. Specifically, we emphasize that local experiences of colonialism, racism and power – as well as local knowledges – share both the meaning of well-being, and the opportunities for it to be realized such" (p. 27).

Considerations for Instructional Design

Due to the results of the pandemic on our educational systems and experiences, it is difficult to ignore the relationship between learning and well-being and how each informs the other. As such, health and well-being need to be built into our pedagogical approaches so that the well-being of learners and instructors are considered in the design of the learning spaces from the beginning. For instructional design, we must consider the factors that support the development of healthy learning environments and overall health and well-being of learners. Drawing back to Andrews' (2017a) assertion that, " 'people make places' and 'places make people' " (p. 44) and health geography's key tenet that "place matters" to health and health care (Kearns & Collins, 2010), intentionally designing learning spaces that consider the health and well-being of instructors and learners draws health geography into conversation with pedagogy.

PRACTICE ACTIVITY

Well-being Questions and Prompts

The following prompts will help you to bring health and well-being considerations into your practice or your work with instructors or subject matter experts (SME):

1. Once again, take a few minutes to reflect on learning environments or previous learning experiences that supported your well-being. What were the positive elements during those experiences that were health supporting? Reflect on a learning experience that was not healthy. What factors lead to that negative experience?
2. Now review the course learning outcomes and assessments. How can holistic health be built into the course? Can well-being be included as a learning outcome, or can opportunities be created so students can co-create additional learning outcomes that address health?
3. What resources and well-being supports are incorporated into the course to support learners' well-being? For example, check-ins at the beginning of class, mediation moments or breaks throughout, or flexible deadlines.
4. What external well-being resources are provided in the course and how are learners made aware of them? Can they be reinforced and discussed throughout the course or at times during the term when learners might need extra support (e.g., exam period)?
5. Consider how learners can share and support each other's health. For example, can students share resources they find supportive through a discussion board or an editable resource page?

Conclusion

Drawing on the concept of therapeutic landscapes, this chapter has provided a quick introduction to how place, one of the foundational concepts in geography, has been taken up by health geographers to deepen our understanding of health and well-being, and it has provided suggestions for how to

140 Michelle Deborah Majeed

incorporate geographic thinking into instructional design practice. As bell hooks (2003) writes, "Committed acts of caring let all students know that the purpose of education is not to dominate, or prepare them to be dominators, but rather to create the conditions for freedom. Caring educators open the mind, allowing students to embrace a world of knowing that is always subject to change and challenge" (p. 92). Considering the current pandemic and potential future interruptions that may impact how and where we learn, geography can provide us the tools to consider how place matters, how it matters to our learning and teaching, how it matters to our health, and how we can support our well-being in the places we learn and teach.

Reference List

Andrews, G. (2017a). Health and place. In T. Brown, G. Andrews, S. Cummins, B. Greenhough, D. Lewis, & A. Power (Eds.), *Health geographies: A critical introduction* (pp. 39–56). Wiley-Blackwell.

Andrews, G. (2017b). Landscapes of wellbeing. In T. Brown, G. Andrews, S. Cummins, B. Greenhough, D. Lewis, & A. Power (Eds.), *Health geographies: A critical introduction* (pp. 59–75). Wiley-Blackwell.

Cattell, V., Dines, N., Gesler, W., & Curtis, S. (2008). Mingling, observing, and lingering: Everyday public spaces and their implications for wellbeing and social relations. *Health Place, 14*(3), 544–561.

Chakrabarti, R. (2010). Therapeutic networks of pregnancy care: Bengali immigrant women in New York City. *Social Science & Medicine, 71*(2), 362–369.

Conradson, D. (2005). Landscape, care and the relational self: Therapeutic encounters in rural England. *Health & Place, 11*(4), 337–348.

Crandon, L. (1986). Medical dialogue and the political economy of medical pluralism: A case from rural highland Bolivia. *American Ethnologist, 13*(3), 463–476.

Cummins, S., Curtis, S., Diez-Roux, A.V., & Macintyre, S. (2007). Understanding and representing "place" in health research: A relational approach. *Social Science & Medicine 65*, 1825–1838.

Dorn, M., & Laws, G. (1994). Social theory, body politics, and medical geography: Extending Kearns's invitation. *The Professional Geographer, 46*, 106–110.

Doughty, K. (2018). Therapeutic landscapes. In P. Howard, I. Thompson, E. Waterton, & M. Atha (Eds.), *The Routledge companion to landscape studies* (2nd ed., pp. 341–353). Routledge.

Eyles, J. (1985). *Senses of place.* Silverbook Press.

Fleuret, S., & Atkinson, S. (2007). Wellbeing, health and geography: A critical review and research agenda. *New Zealand Geographer, 63*(2), 106–118.

Gesler, W. (1996). Lourdes: Healing in a place of pilgrimage. *Health & Place, 2*(2), 95–105.

Gesler, W. (1998). Bath's reputation as a healing place. In R. Kearns & W. Gesler (Eds.), *Putting health into place* (pp. 17–35). Syracuse University Press.

Gesler, W., & Kearns, R.A. (2002). *Culture/place/health.* Routledge.

hooks, b. (2003). *Teaching community: A pedagogy of hope*. Routledge.

Kearns, R.A. (1993). Place and health: Towards a reformed medical geography. *The Professional Geographer, 46*, 67–72.

Kearns, R.A., & Andrews, G.J. (2010). Geographies of wellbeing. In S.J. Smith, R. Pain, S.A. Marston, & J.P. Jones III (Eds.), *Handbook of social geographies* (pp. 309–328). Sage.

Kearns, R.A., & Collins, D. (2010). Health geography. In T. Brown, S. McLafferty, & G. Moon (Eds.), *A companion to health and medical geography* (pp. 15–32). Wiley Online.

Majeed, M.D. (2021). Continuity of care: The ongoing use of "bush medicine" as a transnational therapeutic health practice in Guyanese immigrant communities. *Health & Place, 71*, 102643–102643. https://doi.org/10.1016/j.healthplace.2021.102643

Mayer, J.D., & Meade, M.S. (1994). A reformed medical geography reconsidered. *The Professional Geographer, 46*, 103–106.

Tuan, Y.F. (1979). Space and place: Humanistic perspective. In S. Gale & G. Olsson (Eds.), *Philosophy in geography* (pp. 387–427). Springer.

Tyrell, E., Jeeboo, K., Edmonson-Carter, J., Thomas, T., & Kurup, R. (2020). Attitudes and practices of pharmacists and physicians towards bush medicine in Guyana. *Journal of Complementary and Alternative Medical Research, 11*(4), 1–12.

Williams, A. (2002). Changing geographies of care: Employing the concept of therapeutic landscapes as a framework in examining home space. *Social Science & Medicine, 55*, 141–154.

World Health Organization. (1948). *Preamble to the constitution of the world health organization as adopted by the international health conference, New York.* https://apps.who.int/gb/bd/PDF/bd47/EN/constitution-en.pdf

STEM and Instructional Design   9

A Discussion of STEM Identity Soft Skills in the Instructional Design Field

Blair Stamper

Blair's Story

Throughout my K-12 years as a student, I excelled in the mathematics and scientific fields. I thrived in classes that required me to think through problems, experiment, fail, learn from experiences, and collaborate with my peers. My past successes in science-related fields and my award-winning computer animated design (CAD) drawings led me to consider a degree in the field of engineering. I wanted to solve the world's problems by designing new cars and airplanes that could help society in ways we had never imagined. I had the desire to better the world one design at a time. Around this time, the Great Recession of 2008 was in full swing. Graduating from a metro Detroit high school in 2007, I ultimately saw many of my classmates' successful parents being laid off from their jobs as car engineers. I began envisioning difficulty in proving myself as a female engineer along with a fear of being unable to find a job after college graduation. These circumstances led me to stray away from the final engineering course my high school offered and instead enroll in child development my senior year. Interestingly, this small change completely

DOI: 10.4324/9781003268413-9

transformed my entire life projection. Through the associated internship, I saw a need for female math and science teachers and jumped at the chance to instill a love for these subjects in my students. My desire to better the world was still strong and was integrated into my daily interactions with my students. I strived to create math relevant to their own lives, science more engaging and active, and also connect with my students to help build relationships and get to know them as people rather than just my students. After three long years of pouring myself into my work and being assigned to teach different subjects each year, I was at my mental breaking point. I loved the world of education, including being able to make a daily difference in the lives of my students, and grow myself as a better teacher each year. After months of research and applying to every job possible, I fell into an instructional design position by mistake. I had no clue what this field consisted of, nor how it fit into the greater picture of education. However, I learned quickly that the skills learned throughout my years of loving science and math would help mold me to be a successful instructional designer.

Identity

Before diving into specific experiences, skills, and characteristics, I want to quickly discuss identity. Identity theory traces back to George Herbert Mead's work in *Mind, Self, and Society from the Standpoint of a Social Behaviorist.* An identity is heavily influenced by the environment in which you live and the people in which you interact with on a daily basis (Mead & Morris, 1934; Schunk, 2012). Your achievements and behaviors can also influence how you view yourself within certain situations and can impact your choices later in life (Stryker & Burke, 2000). Building an identity involves taking an inventory of yourself through self-reflection and self-categorization of the skills and characteristics that define you (Stets & Burke, 2000). The underlying root of developing an identity is the recognition of yourself in a role and the comparison of that recognition to specific "meanings and expectations associated with that role" (p. 225). In many cases, these self-views are based upon your interactions in certain groups and communities. This is often referred to as social identity. When your thoughts, beliefs, and behaviors match a certain group or community, you often associate your identity with that group; if they do not align, your identity will not incorporate that group or community (Stets & Burke, 2000).

Given my background as a science and math teacher, my identity often aligns with colleagues in the science, technology, engineering, and mathematics (STEM) field. STEM identity is a sub-theory of identity, social identity, and science identity (Carlone & Johnson, 2007; Dou & Cian, 2021; Starr et al., 2020). Similar to the tenets of identity and social identity, STEM identity is heavily influenced by how you view yourself compared to colleagues and accomplishments within the STEM field (Carlone & Johnson, 2007; Dou & Cian, 2021; Starr et al., 2020). Due to my identification with colleagues associated with the STEM community, I have adopted many STEM characteristics into my identity and applied them daily in instructional design.

This chapter takes a unique approach to defining six specific soft skills that are associated with having a STEM identity. To begin, I define each soft skill and describe how they show up in my own life to help you visualize how you may already have this skill. Next, I will describe how these skills are used in the instructional design field. Finally, I will present a specific scenario I have encountered as an instructional designer and encourage you to use your own STEM identity to solve the problem. As you work through these scenarios, I encourage you to reflect upon your own scientific experiences and how they may fit into the world of instructional design.

Applying STEM Identity to the Instructional Design Field

Science can be defined as a "logical approach to discovering how things work in the universe" (Bradford, 2022). Many of the soft skills/characteristics that I have obtained and honed with a STEM identity have helped me become a successful instructional designer. While there are many soft skills that help me in my day-to-day work, in this chapter I will focus on four of these skills: thinking independently, resilience and perseverance, problem-solving and critical thinking, and collaboration.

Thinking Independently in the STEM Field

People with the ability to think independently are analytical, abstract thinkers. They view events and situations in unique ways by bringing their own perspectives and experiences to form opinions and solutions. Often, independent thinkers do not go with the dominant group flow, rather they propose their own ideas and solutions to the group. Independent thinkers love to learn and expand their knowledge in certain areas to become experts. This mindset allows them to constantly be ahead of possible roadblocks and be thinking

STEM and Instructional Design   **145**

proactively rather than reactively. In addition to these skills, independent thinkers also use their voice to ensure their viewpoint is heard. This allows for further discussion among group members that can often improve processes and final products.

Transferring the Skill to Instructional Design

Instructional designers are leaders. Every team I have worked on as an instructional designer has always been one to push boundaries. We often foresee problems for students and propose solutions before they even become an issue. With each project, we embark on an adventure to lead clients to create a course from nothing or from face-to-face to a fully functional, engaging, and interactive online course. More than likely, the client will have little to no experience with online learning. Using your voice and ability to think independently, it is essential to brainstorm and propose solutions to your clients. This can often mean going against the flow of what has always been done and showcasing how an alternative and innovative idea could create a better overall product and educational experience for the learner.

Strategies for Improving Independent Thinking

Pause

One of the best pieces of advice I received many years ago was "You don't have to be the first one to speak to make the greatest impact." In meetings with clients and/or groups of people, we often think about what we will say next rather than really listening to what is being said and presented. By pausing before speaking, you allow yourself time to think through the different responses and formulate a plan and a response that aligns with the conversation and integrates your own experiences using your voice.

Take Notes

Conversations in meetings can move quickly. One way to implement a pause is by creating a system for taking brief notes. This system should contain shorthand representations for longer words or phrases. For example, students can be written as "Ss" and teachers as "Ts." If you are a visual person, you may also draw pictures or concept maps to represent what is being discussed. Writing while listening forces you to think through the different perspectives of each person. It may also allow you to make connections others may not have seen or proposed.

Schedule a Follow-up

There is a common misconception that solutions should be decided by the end of a meeting. It is OK to pause and reflect if you aren't sure if a solution is truly aligned with the problem or if you need time to reflect. Let the group know that you need time to sit with the information and send a follow-up email, chat, or schedule a meeting directly at the end of the meeting. Not only does this give you a chance to think through all the solutions, but it also holds you accountable to close the loop on the conversation.

Expand your Interactions

Much of our voices and our independent thinking rely upon our own experiences and the people we interact with in our work. Use your network to expand the types of people and interactions you encounter. By getting to know peers with different perspectives, you expand your knowledge and will be able to apply these new experiences to potential conversations in the future.

Start or Join a Book Club

One thing I have learned from working with instructional designers from all over the world is we love to read and learn. When we read a book individually, we apply our own experiences and perspectives to the content of the book. When we read a book with a group of others, we can discuss it and see how the content of the book was interpreted by others. This helps expand your knowledge and visualize alternative ways of doing something that may have been missed. There are many book clubs available for instructional designers through professional memberships, including Online Learning Consortium, Educause, and UPCEA. Don't hesitate to start your own book club as well.

STEM and Instructional Design **147**

Network on Social Media

Using social media professionally expands opportunities and allows for networking with people all over the world. In some ways, these become communities of practice where instructional designers can share their own knowledge, provide guidance, and expand their skill set. Additionally, creating a network helps you to surround yourself with positive, like-minded people. When you do this, you will be able to draw upon the positive energy of your network as you face adversities. Use this network to share ideas, motivate yourself in the right direction, and help you move past challenges you face.

- Twitter Chats: Participate in Twitter chats, such as #ID2IDchat. Twitter chats are a simple and easy way to discuss common problems in instructional design, share experiences, and meet others in the field.
- LinkedIn: Create a LinkedIn profile to connect with other instructional designers and access potential job opportunities.
- Facebook Groups: Instructional design Facebook groups are a great way to search for common challenges and explore what others have done in the same situation.

PRACTICE ACTIVITY

Diversity, Equity, and Inclusion

Scenario: As an instructional designer, it is our duty to ensure that all students are represented in their online course and the content is accessible to everyone. We often get caught up in the idea that accessibility is only for a small percentage of students, but it isn't. In this scenario, you have been tasked with presenting to the online learning team the importance of accessibility and list three easy ways to apply to your institution's online courses. Use your voice and ability to think outside of what always has been done.

   Your Assignment: Using your professional network on social media and in the workplace, and/or scholarly research articles, define accessibility. Why is it important? Who does it impact? How can it impact students' experiences in the online classroom? Then, brainstorm three easy ways to make online courses accessible to all students. Create a video, infographic, or handout using your own voice to present a solution. See the end of the chapter for my own solution.

Add to your portfolio: This is a very real scenario facing instructional designers right now. After you have created your brief synopsis and list of three easy ways to apply accessibility to an online course, be sure to add it to your portfolio for future interviews!

Resilience and Perseverance in the STEM Field

Resilience is the ability to bounce back after challenges while perseverance is the ability to work through those challenges without giving up. Both of these characteristics together create a mindset that promotes trying new things, failing, adjusting, and doing it again. As a STEM teacher, I was always trying new hands-on, active learning strategies to help students learn certain concepts. When these lessons failed or lasted only 10 minutes of the class, I had to reflect and think quickly to try something new or extend the learning. Often, the lessons I thought would be horrible were some of my best, and those that I had spent a ton of time planning were a flop. Using my resilience and perseverance, I was able to adapt quickly and reflect to improve the course for my next group of students.

Transferring the Skill to Instructional Design

Each project as an instructional designer comes with its own set of challenges and roadblocks. You may encounter a project that does not have any established learning objectives, has little to no content, and/or zero assessments created. Or you may work with a subject matter expert who has minimal experience with online learning. Finally, you may encounter roadblocks with a technology that you are working with for a project. During tough projects, it is important to use your perseverance to work through the project and try new things. This might mean drawing upon the knowledge of your other instructional designers to problem-solve new solutions or trying a new working strategy while working with your client. One positive of the instructional design field is the quick turnover of projects. As you are working through a tougher project, it is important to remember that they will eventually end, and you will get to work on a new fresh project. This mindset and experiences with tough projects will help with your resilience and make you a better experienced instructional designer.

Strategies for Improving Resilience and Perseverance

Learn to Fail

People who avoid failure often rarely take chances causing a lack of experimenting and thinking outside of the box. Once you learn to fail, your work will become better. You will thrive being able to experiment, try new things, and then reflect on successes and failures in the process. The most important part of taking chances is the reflection that occurs afterwards. Without this reflection, you may not see certain patterns or epiphanies occurring each time you try something new.

Set Clear Goals

When you see your destination clearly, it is easier to overcome obstacles. Set yourself up for success by not only creating clear goals, but also sub-goals and milestones that will help you reach those goals. A common approach to setting goals is the use of SMART goals. A SMART goal is

- Specific: What are the details of your goal? How can you visualize the goal?
- Measurable: How will you know when you have truly accomplished your goal?
- Achievable: Is the goal really attainable within the time frame specified?
- Relevant: How does the goal align with who or where you want to be in the future?
- Time-Bound: When do you want to accomplish your goal?

Once you have created your SMART goals, post them in an area where you will see them consistently, such as on your bathroom mirror, a bulletin board in your office, or on a bedside table. This will help remind you of these goals and keep you on track to attain them.

Start Small

As you work towards reaching and accomplishing your SMART goal, take small chances to grow your confidence. For example, if your goal is to present at a conference within the next year, start submitting proposals to small, local gatherings. Being accepted to present at a small conference can help build your confidence to present at larger conferences with greater audiences. Additionally, it is an opportunity to share your presentation multiple times and improve each time.

Practice Gratitude

Start each day with 10 minutes of silence. In this silence, think about three things you are grateful for in that moment and write them in a journal. Reflect on these areas of gratitude as you face adversities and challenges throughout the day. Examples of gratitude include:

- I am grateful for the sun rising.
- I am grateful for moving my body today.
- I am grateful for a day without meetings.
- I am grateful for presenting at a conference.

PRACTICE ACTIVITY

The Inexperienced Subject Matter Expert

Scenario: You are working with a subject matter expert (SME) whose project is to be completed over a 16-week period. After the first 4 weeks, it was clear that the course would not meet that deadline. The SME has minimal experience with online learning and has always relied upon organic conversations in the classroom rather than lesson planning. This means the client has no tangible content besides a textbook that could be built into a course. Additionally, the SME often does not have the work you assigned completed at each meeting.

> **Your Assignment:** Knowing your SME only has 12 more weeks to complete their course, how would you approach working with this SME for the remaining time? How could you use setting clear goals to help meet the deadline? See the end of the chapter for my own solution.
>
> Add to your portfolio: This scenario is actually one from my own experiences working with SMEs. In most instructional design interviews, you will be asked a question similar to "Tell me about a time when you worked with someone who didn't meet deadlines and/or wasn't familiar with online learning. How did you approach this SME?"

Using this scenario, you will not be prepared with a specific plan for working with an unresponsive and inexperienced subject matter expert.

Problem-Solving and Critical Thinking in the STEM Field

Scientists often work within systems and processes such as the scientific method to solve problems and think critically. You may remember being introduced to the scientific method back in your science elementary class. You probably conducted small experiments using step-by-step directions to figure out how things worked, answer questions, and make observations about the world. In the real world, the scientific method is used on a larger scale beginning with a question that stems from a problem or an observation. It is important to note that problem-solving is not just a presentation of an issue and coming up with a solution. It takes critical thinking skills to identify a problem, research the cause, test out possible solutions, and reflect on what went well and challenges you faced.

Transferring the Skill to Instructional Design

If you are like me, you probably continue to ask yourself "why" on a daily basis and/or see problems all around you. You may have gleaned from my

152 Blair Stamper

discussions already, but instructional designers and teams are just big groups of problem-solvers. Each project comes with its own set of challenges, roadblocks, and what feel like wicked problems, or a problem with no actual solution, just attempts at solving (Rittel & Webber, 1973). With my STEM identity, I tend to look at every roadblock or challenge as something I can solve. I ask myself, "What solution will help to make a better experience for students and allow all of them to succeed in their studies?" Oftentimes, my initial solution may not work out or the subject matter experts want to go in a different direction. My experiences have taught me that for every problem to have three to five solutions ready to present. This takes research skills, brainstorming, creativity, and critical thinking skills to determine the best aligned solutions possible.

Strategies for Improving Problem-Solving and Critical Thinking Skills

Use Visual Cues

When you're deep in project creation, you can get bogged down by all of the pieces that must come together. This can make you too close to the project and unable to see possible solutions. Create visuals such as mind maps, brain dumps, and curriculum maps to help you see how it all connects. To-do lists in Google Docs can also help you as you develop projects. This can be shared with all stakeholders as you work through all of the different components. As each stakeholder completes pieces, they can be checked or highlighted as being completed.

Know When to Walk Away

This skill is very similar to being able to pause as an independent thinker. You can't be a walking problem-solver. Your brain can short circuit if you attempt to solve too many problems in a short amount of time. This can lead to burnout and frustration. You must know when you have to walk away from the project. Start working on a different project, go for a walk, or read a book. This will help your brain reset and help you see new solutions when you return.

Progress Tracker:

Module	To-Do

Start Here!	• Meet Your Instructor
	  o Update with image and information about yourself
	• Weekly Schedule
	  o Review
	• Important Course Information
	  o Review
	• Grading and Feedback
	  o Review
	• Communication Policies
	  o Review and update for discussion and peer review
	• Student Support and Help
	  o Needs to be updated
	• Discussion: Ask a Question
	• Syllabus
	• Left Menu bar

Week 1	• Encryption Example o Johnny's encryption link? • Double check rubrics • Remove usability activity

Week 2	• Mental Models
	  o Video
	• PowerPoint Slides
	• Accessibility
	• Folk Models
	  o Folk Models of Home Computer Security.

Figure 9.1 Project progress tracker

PRACTICE ACTIVITY

The Inexperienced Subject Matter Expert

Scenario: You are working with a faculty member who has never taught online before. Their course is based on exploration and discussion in a face-to-face course. This often occurs four to five times a week. The instructor wants to make sure that this pattern continues in the online course but isn't sure how to do it. As the instructional designer, you know that four to five discussion boards in a module would be too much for a student (and the faculty member to grade).

Your Assignment: Draft three to four solutions for how you can make the faculty member's course engaging and interactive for students while not overwhelming them all. Build a possible solution in a learning management system (LMS) as an example.

Add to your portfolio: You now have experience with problem-solving using your critical thinking skills. Reflect on how you can use these skills in answering interview questions, specifically related to any challenges you may face while working with a SME. If you took the next step and built a possible solution, you now have a great example to showcase to possible employers!

Collaboration in the STEM Field

Working collaboratively in the STEM field is more than just working with your colleagues on a day-to-day basis. It is the ability to work on a global level. Many companies in the STEM field have offices all over the world. This means projects may include people with different backgrounds, perspectives, cultures, and experiences. Being able to work collaboratively with a diverse group of people is essential. Having greater diversity and participation on projects and feedback can help determine solutions to problems that would not have been reached without multiple perspectives coming together.

Transferring the Skill to Instructional Design

The field of instructional design is extremely collaborative, both between you and other instructional designers, but also between you and the client. In most fields, you will work with a team of instructional designers, each working on different projects. This collaboration between IDs is a great way to share experiences, bounce ideas and research off, and discuss possible solutions. Without these teams and conversations, you are often left with your own experiences and perspectives for problem-solving, which can limit your

STEM and Instructional Design   **155**

potential solutions. For each project, you will work closely with a client to ensure that the final product is portrayed in the way that is best for the learner, but also meets the goals of the client. This can often mean making compromises and having tough conversations. Being able to work closely with multiple stakeholders is essential in the instructional design field.

Strategies for Improving Collaboration Skills

Actively Listen

It was presented earlier how easy it is for us to be thinking about what we are going to say next rather than actually listening. Rather than focusing on how you will respond, take the time to listen to your colleagues in meetings and interactions. Actively listening can mean making eye contact, nodding your head, showing empathy and interest and acknowledging what was said. In your response you can use phrases such as "If I understand correctly . . .," or "Just to clarify, are you saying . . ." These can show the colleague that you are truly listening and attempting to decipher what they are trying to say.

Set Clear Expectations

One of the most important aspects of teamwork and collaboration is that there are no shining stars. Instead, you succeed and fail as a team. Setting clear expectations within teams (even between two people) is important for success. Each team member must hold one another accountable to meet deadlines, and there must be a feeling of a safe space to be able to share ideas. In one to one projects, set these expectations early to help allow all team members to shine together and create a well-functioning team. Use your first meeting as a way to get to know one another and create a calendar of deadlines together.

PRACTICE ACTIVITY

The Siloed SME

Scenario: You are working at a higher education institution that incorporates cohorts throughout the course design and development process. Each semester, there are approximately 15–20 faculty members working with 4–5 instructional designers. While all of the instructional designers meet regularly, faculty members rarely get to meet one another. Because of this, all of the courses are often built in silos between you and the faculty member. Ideas are then transferred from ID to ID rather than shared among faculty members.

Your Assignment: Create a plan for how to increase collaboration between the 15–20 faculty members. How can you create more cohesiveness among them, especially those in the same department? How can you help ideas transfer from faculty to faculty? See the end of the chapter for my own solution.

Add to your portfolio: You guessed it. This is another scenario that is actually one from my own experiences working on courses with SMEs. Working through this scenario will help you build specific ideas and examples for creating a better community among each cohort of SMEs.

Pulling it All Together

In this chapter, you were presented with four soft skills that people with a STEM identity often embody and how to utilize them in the instructional design field. Now you too have the knowledge and strategies for using these skills in your own work with tangible examples that can be integrated into your own portfolio. I encourage you to begin integrating these strategies into your own day-to-day work to help become the best version of yourself and in your work as an instructional designer!

Scenario Solutions

Scenario: Diversity, Equity, and Inclusion

Putting closed captioning on videos allows students to read while listening or watching. Adding alt tags on pictures and using pictures that enhance learning rather than using decorative images allows students with screen readers to get the full experience of the content. Being aware of font choices and color contrast can also help students with reading the content with technology not being a barrier to learning.

Scenario: The Inexperienced Subject Matter Expert

Many years ago, I worked with a client whose project was to be completed over a 16-week period. After the first 4 weeks, it was clear that the course would not meet that deadline. The client had minimal experience with online learning and relied upon organic conversations in the classroom for teaching. This meant the client had no tangible content besides a textbook that could be built into a course. The project was then extended to 32 weeks with me struggling to get the client to meet deadlines. During that time, I had to use multiple strategies while working with the client, including setting up working meetings, creating the course format on my own, and building out the course based on the textbook. There were many opportunities when I could have given up, but my perseverance and passion for student success would not let me. The final product was definitely not one of my most successful projects, but the course was completed, and students were able to attend online to complete their degree.

Scenario: The Siloed SME

In higher education we work in cohorts throughout the course design and development process. Each semester, there are 15–20 faculty members working with approximately 4–5 instructional designers. This work is often done in silos between the instructional designer and the faculty member without a sense of community. To help remedy this at one institution, I created a cohort, where faculty members could meet together two to three times throughout the semester-long project. These conversations among the faculty members opened up doors for multi-disciplinary collaboration, sharing of experiences, and helping faculty see that they were not alone in this adventure. The process became a more positive experience for all involved and allowed for new ideas to be integrated into the online courses that may never have come to fruition without these collaborative meetings. It also gave the instructional designers new perspectives and a sense of comradery between the IDs and the faculty members.

Reference List

Bradford, A. (2022). *Science and the scientific method: Definitions and examples*. Live Science. www.livescience.com/20896-science-scientific-method.html

Carlone, H.B., & Johnson, A. (2007). Understanding the science experiences of successful women of color: Science identity as an analytic lens. *Journal of Research in Science Teaching*, 44(8), 1187–1218. https://doi.org/10.1002/tea.20237

Dou, R., & Cian, H. (2021). Constructing STEM identity: An expanded structural model for STEM identity research. *Journal of Research in Science Teaching*. https://doi.org/10.1002/tea.21734

Mead, G.H., & Morris, C. (1934). *Mind, self & society from the standpoint of a social behaviorist*. University of Chicago Press.

Rittel, H.W., & Webber, M.M. (1973). Dilemmas in a general theory of planning. *Policy Sciences*, 4(2), 155–169.

Schunk, D.H. (2012). *Learning theories an educational perspective* (6th ed.). Pearson.

Starr, C.R., Hunter, L., Dunkin, R., Honig, S., Palomino, R., & Leaper, C. (2020). Engaging in science practices in classrooms predicts increases in undergraduates' STEM motivation, identity, and achievement: A short-term longitudinal study. *Journal of Research in Science Teaching*, 57(7), 1093–1118. https://doi.org/10.1002/tea.21623

Stets, J.E., & Burke, P.J. (2000). Identity theory and social identity theory. *Social Psychology Quarterly*, 63(3), 224–237.

Stryker, S., & Burke, P.J. (2000). The past, present, and future of an identity theory. *Social Psychology Quarterly*, 63(4), 284–297.

Lessons From the Barre

10

The Intersection Between Dance and Dynamic Instructional Design Decision-Making

Jill E. Stefaniak

Jill's Story

It is an adrenaline rush like no other! The first 20 seconds on stage are the longest. You are immersed in total darkness. You feel your heart pumping louder and louder as you wait for what seems like an eternity. Then the curtains open, the music starts, the stage lights come on, and you are dancing! You have three minutes to tell your audience a story through music and movement. You perform a series of steps, one flowing into the next. You're careful as you maneuver around the other dancers on the stage during formation and line changes and try to remember the facial expressions needed to express what's happening in the dance.

Everything that you have been working hard to accomplish is showcased in a few minutes that feels like mere seconds. Depending on the brightness of the lights, you may or may not see your audience. But you know that they are there. By the time you reach the end, the audience erupts in applause. Your

DOI: 10.4324/9781003268413-10

160 Jill E. Stefaniak

adrenaline kicks in again. You hope that you've remembered everything and that you performed the routine the same way you did earlier in rehearsals.

It was not until I became a professor and started teaching classes related to human performance technology, program evaluation, and needs assessment that I realized how much my previous experience with dance was influencing my work as a practitioner, teacher, and researcher. As an instructor, I was often describing how I approached previous design projects. I realized that a lot of what I was describing in class mirrored how I approached choreography. In essence, I was choreographing design strategies – coordinating different instructional events, scaling activities based on time and money, and aligning the needs of different stakeholders. My experience with choreography was influencing how I made design decisions, oftentimes, considering environmental factors, resources, and different stakeholders involved with projects.

Introduction

The purpose of this chapter is to discuss how dance education can influence instructional design practice. I will address the synergy between goals of instructional design and goals for choreography in dance. I will then provide an overview of systems and how the prevalence of systems thinking in dance translates to instructional design practices. I will conclude by providing recommendations for how the intersection between dance and instructional design can support designers' dynamic decision-making.

Systems thinking involves compartmentalizing the environment that you are interacting within, providing a means to explore how dynamic components of a system (people, objects, processes) interact and impact possible outcomes (Cabrera & Cabrera, 2019). It requires you to look at the larger picture and the multiple layers that comprise a system and work to ensure alignment between different stakeholders (i.e., employees, learners, teachers, administrators) within that system.

The Choreography of Instructional Design

While many different definitions are referenced in the field of learning, design, and technology, I tend to gravitate toward Richey et al.'s (2011) definition that "instructional design is the science and art of creating detailed specifications for the development, evaluation, and maintenance of situations which facilitate learning and performance" (p. 3). Other definitions describe instructional design as being a systematic process where an instructional designer navigates through various phases of a project to analyze, design, develop, implement, and evaluate (Dick et al., 2005; Smith & Ragan, 2005). It is important to recognize that while systematic suggests a process, it does not necessarily mean that it must promote linearity.

Instructional design is very much an iterative process where an instructional designer must be continuously reviewing various aspects of the design phase, the learning and transfer contexts, and any additional information that may be introduced to the project (Tessmer & Wedman, 1990). If the purpose of instructional design is to create detailed specifications that facilitate learning and improve performance, it is essential that instructional designers understand with great clarity the situation that they are designing within and for. If we were generalizing the goals of instructional design, we could safely assume that all instructional design projects want to meet the needs of their learning audience through sustainable means of instruction and support. These goals, regardless of context, necessitate an understanding of the *big picture*.

Choreography is described by dancers as "a referent for a structuring of movement, not necessarily the movement of human beings" (Foster, 2011, p. 8). Several dance educationists describe the profession of choreography as assembling a series of actions to be performed in a desired progression (Butterworth, 2004; Hagood & Kahlich, 2007; Lavender, 2009; Risner, 2000; Van Dyke, 2005). This very much aligns with general systems theory which takes into consideration how various components diverge and converge in a system.

Things became increasingly complex when I had to choreograph dance routines that involved multiple dancers. I had to consider how my dancers would enter and exit the stage. How could I move them around the stage and change formations without them running into each other or getting in one another's way? I had to be careful that I was not distracting the audience with having too many different things occur on stage at the same time. How could I use my dancers' strengths to showcase their abilities and talents as dancers? How could I compensate for dancers who may be weaker than others when performing certain dance movements? In many ways, the above-mentioned questions required me to appreciate the system that I was designing with and leverage the strengths of individuals within the system.

162 Jill E. Stefaniak

Instructional Design as a System

In its most primitive sense, a system is composed of "a set of objects together with relationships between the objects and between their attributes" (Hall & Fagen, 1975, p. 52). Systems can be open where various components interact within and across subsystems of a larger system and environment. They can also be considered closed where components within the system are isolated from other components in the system and environment (von Bertalanffy, 1968).

It is important to note that every system, regardless of whether it is a living organism, instructional system, or organizational system, has a certain degree of entropy (chaos) and self-regulating processes (Skyttner, 2001). The degree of transformation is dependent on the relationship between entropy and self-regulation. These two variables have an inverse relationship; when entropy or chaos is high in an organization, the system's ability to self-regulate will be low. When thinking about learning and performance in instructional settings (i.e., K-12 schools, higher education institutions, or corporate settings), "systems that utilize self-regulating processes typically mitigate entropy that can constrain the transformation processes needed for the system to achieve its goal(s)" (Stefaniak, 2021a, p. 52).

In their book, *The Instructional Design Knowledge Base: Theory, Research, and Practice*, Richey et al. (2011) discuss the components of a general system as they relate to instructional design. They recognize that environments are comprised of systems that may have additional subsystems. Regardless of the layering that may exist in the overarching environment, each system is comprised of interactions that occur within and between persons, processes, and objects. Persons may include the instructional designers, educators, learners, and other constituents who may have an interest in the goals of the system. Processes include steps for completing the goals of the organization. Per an instructional design lens, this may include systematic processes used to design and develop instruction as well as expected procedures that exist to support the system's (e.g., school or organization) ability to self-regulate.

Systems can be considered dynamic in that they continuously evolve and change over time (Richardson & Chemero, 2014). Dynamic systems are open systems in that there is a high degree of interactivity that takes place between the components that comprise the system (Beer, 2000). Change may emerge because of interactions occurring between components of the system (Richardson & Chemero, 2014). When changes occur, a system can self-regulate and work towards its intended purpose when less chaos is involved. Table 10.1 provides examples of how system components are addressed in choreography and instructional design.

PRACTICE ACTIVITY

Identifying Dynamic System Elements

Think about an instructional design project you are currently completing or have recently completed. If you were to envision the project from start to finish as a performance on stage, how would you account for the different dynamic system elements. Use the questions in Table 10.1 to guide you as you begin to map out how you would choreograph your instructional design project.

Table 10.1 Questions to support instructional designers' understanding of their instructional design system

Dynamic Systems Element	Considerations for Choreography	Questions to be Considered by the Instructional Designer
Purpose	• What message is the choreographer trying to convey to the audience through dance?	• What is the system's (i.e., school, organization, etc.) function? • What is the purpose of the instructional design project?
Interactivity between components	• To what extent, do dancers interact and engage with one another in the performance?	• Who/what comprises the system? • To what extent do individuals within the system interact with one another? • Does conflict exist between the different components (i.e., people, processes) in the system?

164 Jill E. Stefaniak

Dynamic Systems Element	Considerations for Choreography	Questions to be Considered by the Instructional Designer
Degrees of entropy	• What errors or mistakes occur during the dance performance? • What were the implications of these mistakes?	• Are there any problems or tensions that may interfere with the success of the instructional design project? • How long has entropy existed within the system? • Have root causes been identified?
Self-regulating mechanisms	• What rules and norms have been established for the dancers to follow during the dance performance? • How do the dancers flow from one dance sequence to the next?	• What processes are in place to support the daily functions of the system? • Are the current processes working? • Are certain processes needed to support new instructional design solutions that are expected to be developed? • Who is responsible for implementing new processes within the organization?

Historically, instructional design and human performance technology frameworks are grounded in general systems theory. Seels and Richey (1994) acknowledged the systemic nature of instructional design by describing it as "a systematic approach to the design, production, evaluation, and utilization of complete systems of instruction, including all appropriate components and a management pattern for using them" (p. 172). Their recognition of a need for managing the components within a system stipulates the need for appropriate interaction and progression through the various phases of instruction design. When we think of instructional systems and dynamic systems, the ability to self-regulate can be attributed to individuals' understanding and adherence to policies and procedures that help govern the system and promote productivity.

Choreographing within a Dynamic System

Reflecting on various instructional design projects that I have worked on throughout my career, I recognize that the systems were dynamic. When instructional designers employ a recursive and iterative approach to instructional design, they are designing within a dynamical system. Wilson (2002) suggests that dynamic systems are situated, time-pressured, and require a degree of off-loading to support the individuals and components within the system. These characteristics are prevalent in both dance and instructional design.

Managing Space

It is important to consider the interconnectedness between components of a system. Dance choreographers work to organize a series of movements in a progression that takes into consideration use of space, messaging, and time. Smith (2012) describes this process as a "rich and dynamic verbal and non-verbal dialogue between a choreographer and their extraordinary dancer" (p. 8). We can liken this to the relationship between an instructional designer and their learning audience. If an instructional designer understands the system and the context in which their project is situated, they are more likely to develop solutions that will mitigate entropy and support the learners' and other stakeholders' abilities to self-regulate within the system.

When I was a dance student, I had to think about how best to use my stage to tell a story. Where dancers would be positioned on stage would convey a different message to the audience. If my dancers were front and

166 Jill E. Stefaniak

center on stage, that would indicate they were confident and wanted to be seen. They might use large movements and motions with their arms and legs to demonstrate full use of the space around them. If the purpose of the dance was to convey shyness, dancers might be backed towards the back corner of the stage where they would use smaller movements to convey their vulnerability.

The same expectations occur while you are designing instruction. When an instructional designer begins a project, designers may start planning through the ADDIE (analysis, design, development, implementation, and evaluation) process. This might be compared to a choreographed event on a larger stage. In dance, dancers will enter the stage at different points in a dance routine. This can be likened to stakeholders entering instructional design projects at various times. The amount of time that a stakeholder may be involved directly with the project is variable.

Table 10.1 provides you a list of questions to help you better understand any complexities that may exist within the system before you begin designing instruction. Once you have gathered answers to those questions, you can then start thinking about how each component will be introduced to the project. Table 10.2 provides a list of questions you may consider when mapping out your space for your design project once you have conducted a needs assessment and have a better understanding of the situation.

PRACTICE ACTIVITY

Mapping Design Projects

Mapping out an instructional design project has a lot of similarities to choreographing a dance. We have to consider when different individuals may become involved with the project no different than when a choreographer plans how dancers will enter and exit the stage for a performance. Once you have identified an instructional project, you can begin mapping out how individuals (i.e., instructional designers, learners, team members, and/or other stakeholders) may enter various phases of the project. The questions in Table 10.2 are meant to guide your decisions for how your project will be designed and implemented through the system.

Table 10.2 Questions to support mapping out instructional design projects

Phase of Project	Possible Questions
Planning Design	• Who in the organization needs to be involved to provide feedback on initial design questions? • Are there subject matter experts the instructional designer will have access to during the project? • How will feedback be obtained throughout the design and development of the project? • Which stakeholders will be impacted (directly or indirectly) by the ID materials?
Development	• Are there particular individuals who need to provide feedback on the developed ID materials before implementation? • What is the timeline for development? • How much time is available to receive feedback and make modifications?
Implementation	• Is there a phased plan for rolling out instructional materials to stakeholders? • What is the timeline for implementation? • Which stakeholders need to be evolved in decisions regarding implementation?
Evaluation	• What evaluative mechanisms are in place to ensure the instructional materials addressed their intended purpose? • Who will be involved in evaluation? • What are the evaluation periods (i.e., six months, annual)? • Who is responsible for assessing the evaluative data and making revisions/recommendations for future instructional design needs? • Which stakeholders need to be evolved in decisions regarding evaluation?
Maintenance	• Who is responsible for monitoring the project once it is fully launched in the organization? • Which stakeholders need to be evolved in decisions regarding maintenance?

168 Jill E. Stefaniak

In addition to the typical phases commonly included in the ADDIE process, I have added maintenance as a phase for you to consider when engaging in design within a dynamic system. As previously mentioned, dynamic systems can change as different components interact with one another. It is important for you to start planning who will be responsible for monitoring the project once it has been fully launched in the organization. This will help you determine if you are meeting the goals of the project and needs of the system as well as identify if there are any additional areas that may need to be addressed.

Supporting Self-Regulating Instructional Design Systems

Dance is very much a self-regulating system where the dancer must be aware of their body, the space they have available to dance, the rules pertaining to the style of dance, and norms of the dancer team. There are a variety of mechanisms that an instructional designer may consider to support a system's ability to self-regulate to mitigate entropy. Examples may include policies and processes that support the goals of the system. In a learning environment, this may consist of establishing guidelines for how technology may be used to support learning in a classroom, providing learners with technological tools and appropriate training on how to use those tools to support their learning. Policies may be created to provide additional information to learners, if needed. An instructional designer's ability to support the self-regulation of the system (learning environment) is largely dependent on their ability to understand the needs of individuals within the system (Stefaniak, 2021a).

Their ability to intuitively anticipate their learners' needs and needs of the environment are a direct result of their development of expertise in instruction (Ertmer & Stepich, 2005). This is something instructional designers gain with experience in design and familiarity with the dynamical systems they interact with during their projects. Considering that interactions within systems are ongoing and ever-changing, it is important that instructional designers become comfortable with the ability to engage in dynamic decisions.

Engaging in Dynamic Decision-Making

Dancers engage in dynamic decision-making every time they choreograph and perform. They must make swift movements to accompany other dancers on stage. They must be reactive if any unexpected changes occur during a dance routine. This is similar to how instructional designers engage in decisions.

Instructional designers engage in decision-making ongoingly while working on design projects. Decision-making is the process of making choices, weighing options and selecting solutions to support the goals of a project (Jonassen, 2012). Instructional design decisions can be classified as either rational or dynamic. Rational decision-making entails an individual identifying a series of different options, weighing the advantages and disadvantages of each option, and proceeding with a decision (Jonassen, 2011). These types of decisions typically require more time and may or may not involve multiple individuals. Jonassen (2012) purports that these types of decisions are often evaluated based on rational choice, cost-benefit, and risk assessment. Examples of rational decision-making in instructional design may involve a department at a higher education institution deciding to pursue the development of a new degree program, an e-learning department at a corporation modifying their existing online courses to expand their global audience, or a teacher pivoting instruction from a face-to-face to an online environment in response to a pandemic.

Dynamic decision-making involves the process of making choices promptly within a short time frame (Klein, 2008). Instructional designers may not have the luxury to wait for an extended period of time. Dynamic decisions are often made in situ, taking into account the activity occurring in the learning environment (the system) and modifying instructional strategies and activities to support the needs of the learners and the goals of the project (Stefaniak & Xu, 2020; Stefaniak et al., 2021).

When instructional designers engage in dynamic decision-making, they need to be mindful of their system and how various components (i.e., learners, teachers, technological tools) are interacting with one another. Dynamic decisions need to be responsive and adaptive to the needs of the system. Instructional designers are better positioned to make these decisions when they understand the degree of entropy that may exist within the system and the extent that the system is able to self-regulate to meet its goals (Stefaniak, 2021a).

Monitoring Design Flow

Dynamic decision-making elicits creativity in the decision-making process. The decision-maker is responsible for making decisions quickly using the resources and environmental affordances available to them in a given moment. This supports a creative process that considers how objects in the environment contribute or hinder the problem-solving space.

Dance educationists and anthropologists use the term *flow* to describe a personal psychological state of well-being associated with the creative process (Biasutti & Habe, 2021; Hefferon & Ollis, 2006; Jaque et al., 2020; Lepecki, 2006). Different genres of dance are guided by rules that require the learning of skills, goals, and feedback mechanisms "that makes control possible" (Csikszentmihalyi, 1990, p. 72).

What might flow look like for an instructional designer? Instructional design is recognized for being a field that embodies both scientific inquiry yet espouses an artfulness (Clinton & Hokanson, 2012; McDonald et al., 2020). Like different genres of dance, instructional design is guided by a series of principles (Branch & Kopcha, 2014; Dick et al., 2005; Gagné et al., 2005).

Examples of how you may engage in design flow while working as an instructional designer predominantly involve thinking about the various types of transitions that may occur throughout the different phases of the project. Instructional design is an iterative process where you often are required to revisit different aspects of your design plans and new information becomes available or new constraints are presented. Determining when you have *enough* information to move onto the next phase of your project is an example of design flow.

Design flow is also present when you engage in phased rollouts of your project. Every instructional design project is different so it is impossible to say that every instructional designer will engage in design flow the same way. Depending on the project, you may find yourself in discussions about piloting instructional materials with a small audience to obtain their feedback before implementing it to the entire organization. Determining who would comprise the pilot audience and how stakeholders will be introduced to the materials are other examples that would emulate design flow in an instructional system.

We demonstrate design flow every time we make modifications to our projects. Perhaps, our client has had to reduce the timeline or budget for a project. Other examples of modifications that you may find yourself making on a regular basis include changing the scope or focus of particular modules within a course, integrating updated multimedia tools, or making quick changes if an error has been identified at any phase of the project.

While many of these changes may feel intuitive to you because you are used to making modifications to your projects, you are demonstrating creativity and design flow, and you use your instructional design expertise and knowledge of the system to navigate these changes.

Instructional designers have goals for their projects that may address multiple components within a system. These may be specific goals for the learners to accomplish during and after training, organizational goals to support learners' transfer of training, or goals related to mitigating challenges that are inhibiting the system's ability to self-regulate and achieve its goals.

The integration of feedback mechanisms in the system support interactions and provide the components (i.e., people) in the system with the necessary information they need to make change as needed. This is what truly makes instructional systems dynamic in nature. Every instructional design environment offers affordances that either contribute to the success or hinder the goals of instruction (Stefaniak & Xu, 2020). These affordances are proffered by the instructional designers and teachers, learners, and the environment itself.

Instructional designers can customize their designs and incorporate feedback within the system to *make control possible* by recognizing the capabilities and limitations of the individuals within the system. The environmental affordances that an instructional designer must consider when sequencing instruction with appropriate scaffolds is similar to what choreographers must consider when arranging their dances. They must take into consideration the expertise of their dancers, the amount of space they have to use for movement, and the physical constraints imposed on their dancers' bodies when transitioning from movement to movement. In both instances, they need to manage their design space and choreograph within a bounded rationality considering time constraints, their own experience, and the affordances provided to the situation (Simon, 1969).

Key Takeaways Regarding What Instructional Designers Learn from Dance?

Scholars who study dance describe a *state of flow* as becoming one with the group (Lucznik et al., 2020). This is achieved when dancers can regulate their movements seamlessly in perfect coordination. This idea espousing a state of flow in instructional design could support the argument that instruction is dynamic, and the instructional designer is as much a component of the system as the learners and other environmental objects.

I have tried to emulate a state of flow in both my consultative and pedagogical practices to support my dynamic decision-making practices. As a practitioner, I recognize the consultative role I play when designing solutions, both instructional and non-instructional, for an organization. I impose myself on the system during my tenure with that project. I do that intentionally to support my ability to understand the intricacies of their system. I need to understand the extent that entropy is disrupting the system. I need to know how people are adapting and modifying their processes in the wake of entropy. At the same time, I need to understand the self-regulating processes used by the system and identify solutions that do not destroy good processes that are currently working. If instructional designers rely on taking a view of the system from the periphery, they will encounter difficulties creating sustainable solutions for their clients and learning audiences.

As I reflect on my own design practices, I can see how my training in dance has supported my adoption of systems thinking as an instructional designer. The following are strategies I implement regularly in my design projects that stem from my experience and appreciation of dance and systems thinking.

Map Out Your Space

When a choreographer begins to create a dance, they consider the space they have to work with to tell their story. Mapping out their space allows them to determine how their dancer(s) will maneuver through the space to convey a story to the audience. This is where the choreographer may plan for how dancers will enter or exit the stage, formation changes, and the types of movements that will be carried out.

Instructional designers commonly map out their projects using design documents, where they identify key information about their learning audience, goals of instruction, learning objectives, instructional strategies, and means to measure the success of the project (Stefaniak, 2021b). Mapping out your space goes beyond the traditional design document that are familiar to most instructional designers.

The idea of mapping out space helps the instructional designer to acknowledge and establish design constraints for a given project. While the term *constraints* typically has a negative connotation, I argue that instructional designers should use them to their benefit. Constraints provide boundaries for a project. They make it clear how much space and resourcing we have to use in order to design and implement solutions. The types of design constraints imposed on a project ultimately elicit creativity from the instructional designer and help them to engage in dynamic decision-making.

Lessons From the Barre **173**

PRACTICE ACTIVITY

Mapping Your Design Space

One way that you could map out space to address constraints is to create a document that is shared with your design team that addresses the boundaries of the project. This could be a stand-alone document, or you may also choose to add it as an addendum to a design document or plan that your team may be using. Within this document you could make note of design particulars that cannot alter. Examples of some design boundaries may include the following:

- Noting how much time is allocated for design, development, and feedback prior to implementation.
- Addressing what types of technology must be used or what types of technology need to be avoided.
- Technology boundaries such as any requirements for length of e-learning modules, number of pages for print-based materials, what types of multimedia that can or cannot be used, and requirements for hosting materials (i.e., learning management systems, servers).

Anticipate the Flow from Movement to Movement

This chapter previously explored how choreography is a process of assembling a series of actions and movements in a desired progression. In dance, the choreographer considers how one dance movement ends and what needs to happen in order for the next movement to begin. The physicality and flexibility of the dancer(s) need to be considered in addition to their positioning on stage.

Instructional designers engage as choreographers of instruction. As they begin to design instructional activities, they determine appropriate sequencing of activities. Their ability to structure learning activities that build upon their learners' prior knowledge and increase in complexity is quite similar to scaffolding a dance. As they take into consideration their design space and activity occurring within their system (e.g., interactions between system objects,

174 Jill E. Stefaniak

degree of entropy, mechanisms in place to support self-regulation), it is imperative to anticipate the implications of introducing anything new to the system.

Conveying a Story

I previously mentioned that dance involves telling a story within a matter of minutes to an audience. Viewing instructional design as a dance can help instructional designers reflect on the story they want to convey to their learning audience. All instructional experiences are time-sensitive whether it lasts a few minutes in an e-learning module, is a compilation of modules, lasts a semester, or an entire year. When mapping out space, the instructional designer should consider the messaging they wish to convey.

We typically think of message design in terms of how we arrange text and images on computer screens and paper to support learners' information processing. If we extend beyond this and approach instructional design as a choreography, we can enhance our instructional materials by empathizing with our audience and thinking about how we want them to think and feel as they engage in the instructional experience.

Choreographers convey different emotions through specific placements and movements on stage. We can embody a similar approach in our design work by anticipating how our learners may feel while engaging in instruction, the typical struggles they may encounter learning something new, and providing opportunities for them to practice and build their confidence. These instructional design activities are a direct result of us intentionally placing activities on our instructional stage. We engage in dynamic decision-making every time we scan our stage and the components of our system and make modifications to support our audience.

This is something that I try to espouse in the instructional design courses I teach. Regardless of whether I am teaching introductory or advanced instructional design, online instruction, or human performance technology, I intentionally incorporate discussions of systems thinking throughout. Human performance technology literature provides a great foundation for understanding systems thinking and the role that analyses (i.e., gap, causal, environmental) play in guiding the design of instructional and non-instructional interventions. We typically see that infrastructure is acknowledged more often in scholarship that is centered around human performance technology (Foshay et al., 2014). Rather than leaving discussions about infrastructure to the traditional courses on human performance technology and needs assessment, I think it is important to introduce these ideas to students in every design course.

You can accomplish this by taking a 30,000-foot view of your project and asking questions to understand how your design work will transition from idea to design, implementation, and maintenance within the organization. The different tables and suggested questions included in this chapter are meant to serve as a guide to help you ask questions about the role and influence the system will have on your instructional design project.

Conclusion

I strongly believe that instructional designers need to consider infrastructure similar to how a choreographer considers the use of physical space when designing movements for a performance. We need to recognize the systemic nature between components within our system, the implications that movements and design decisions impose on subsequent movements. We need to recognize the role that we play as instructional designers within our systems. We are instruments within those systems. Our abilities to design solutions are inherently dependent on our ability to interact with and evolve with the people, processes, and objects that comprise our systems.

Reference List

Beer, R.D. (2000). Dynamical approaches to cognitive science. *Trends in Cognitive Sciences, 4*(3), 91–99. https://doi.org/10.1016/S1364-6613(99)01440-0

Biasutti, M., & Habe, K. (2021). Teachers' perspectives on dance improvisation and flow. *Research in Dance Education*, 1–20. https://doi.org/10.1080/14647893.2021.1940915

Branch, R.M., & Kopcha, T.J. (2014). Instructional design models. In J.M. Spector, M.D. Merrill, J. Elen, & M.J. Bishop (Eds.), *Handbook of research on educational communications and technology* (4th ed., pp. 77–87). Springer.

Butterworth, J. (2004). Teaching choreography in higher education: A process continuum model. *Research in Dance Education, 5*(1), 45–67. https://doi.org/10.1080/1464789042000190870

Cabrera, D., & Cabrera, L. (2019). What is systems thinking? In M.J. Spector, B.B. Lockee, & M.D. Childress (Eds.), *Learning, design, and technology: An international compendium of theory, research, practice, and policy* (pp. 1–28). Springer.

Clinton, G., & Hokanson, B. (2012). Creativity in the training and practice of instructional designers: The design/creativity loops model. *Educational Technology Research and Development, 60*(1), 111–130. https://doi.org/10.1007/s11423-011-9216-3

Csikszentmihalyi, M. (1990). *Flow: The psychology of optimal experience.* Harper Collins Publishers.

Dick, W., Carey, L., & Carey, L. (2005). *The systematic design of instruction* (6th ed.). HarperCollins.

176 Jill E. Stefaniak

Ertmer, P.A., & Stepich, D.A. (2005). Instructional design expertise: How will we know it when we see it? *Educational Technology, 45*(6), 38–43.

Foshay, W.R., Villachica, S.W., & Stepich, D.A. (2014). Cousins but not twins: Instructional design and human performance technology in the workplace. In J.M. Spector, M.D. Merrill, J. Elen, & M.J. Bishop (Eds.), *Handbook of research on educational communications and technology* (4th ed., pp. 39–49). Springer.

Foster, S.L. (2011). *Choreographing empathy*. Routledge.

Gagné, R.M., Wager, W.W., Golas, K.C., & Keller, J.M. (2005). *Principles of instructional design* (5th ed.). Thomson Wadsworth.

Hagood, T.K., & Kahlich, L.C. (2007). Research in choreography. In *International handbook of research in arts education* (pp. 517–531). Springer.

Hall, A.D., & Fagen, R.E. (1975). Definition of a system. In B.D. Ruben & J.Y. Kin (Eds.), *General systems theory and human communications* (pp. 52–65). Hayden Book Company, Inc.

Hefferon, K., & Ollis, S. (2006). "Just clicks": An interpretive phenomenological analysis of professional dancers' experience of flow. *Research in Dance Education, 7*(2), 141–159. https://doi.org/10.1080/14647890601029527

Jaque, S.V., Thomson, J., Zaragoza, F., Werner, J., Podeszwa, J., & Jacobs, K. (2020). Creative flow and physiologic states in dancers during performance. *Frontiers in Psychology, 11*. https://doi.org/10.3389/fpsyg.2020.01000

Jonassen, D.H. (2011). *Learning to solve problems: A handbook for designing problem-solving learning environments*. Routledge.

Jonassen, D.H. (2012). Designing for decision making. *Educational Technology Research and Development, 60*(2), 341–359. https://doi.org/10.1007/s11423-011-9230-5

Kearns, R.A., & Andrews, G.J. (2010). Geographies of Wellbeing. In S.J. Smith, R. Pain, S.A. Marston, & J.P. Jones III (Eds.), *The SAGE handbook of social geographies* (pp. 309–328). SAGE Publications Ltd.

Klein, G. (2008). Naturalistic decision making. *Human Factors, 50*(3), 456–460.

Lavender, L. (2009). Dialogical practices in teaching choreography. *Dance Chronicle, 32*(3), 377–411. https://doi.org/10.1080/01472520903276735

Lepecki, A. (2006). *Exhausting dance: Performance and the politics of movement*. Routledge.

Lucznik, K., May, J., & Redding, E. (2020). A qualitative investigation of flow experience in group creativity. *Research in Dance Education, 22*(1), 190–209. https://doi.org/10.1080/14647893.2020.1746259

McDonald, J.K., West, R.E., Rich, P.J., & Hokanson, B. (2020). Instructional design for learner creativity. In M. Bishop, E. Boling, J. Elen, & V. Svihla (Eds.), *Handbook of research in educational communications and technology* (5th ed., pp. 375–399). Springer.

Richardson, M.J., & Chemero, A. (2014). Complex dynamical systems and embodiment. In L. Shapiro (Ed.), *The Routledge handbook of embodied cognition* (pp. 57–68). Routledge.

Richey, R.C., Klein, J.D., & Tracey, M.W. (2011). *The instructional design knowledge base: Theory, research, and practice*. Routledge.

Risner, D. (2000). Making dance, making sense: Epistemology and choreography. *Research in Dance Education, 1*(2), 155–172. https://doi.org/10.1080/713694259

Seels, B., & Richey, R. (1994). *Instructional technology: The definitions and domains of the field*. Association for Educational Communications and Technology.

Simon, H.A. (1969). *The sciences of the artificial*. MIT Press.

Skyttner, L. (2001). *General systems theory: Ideas and applications*. World Scientific Publishing.

Smith, P.L., & Ragan, T.J. (2005). *Instructional design* (3rd ed.). Jossey-Bass.

Smith, R.A. (2012). *Creativity, flow, and the dance-muse in choreography* (Unpublished master's thesis). University of California.

Stefaniak, J.E. (2021a). *Needs assessment for learning and performance: Theory, process, and practice*. Routledge.

Stefaniak, J.E. (2021b). Documenting instructional design decisions. In J.K. McDonald & R.E. West (Eds.), *Design for learning: Principles, processes, and praxis*. EdTech Books. https://edtechbooks.org/id/documenting_decisions

Stefaniak, J.E., Luo, T., & Xu, M. (2021). Fostering pedagogical reasoning and dynamic decision-making practices: A conceptual framework to support learning design in a digital age. *Educational Technology Research and Development, 69*(4), 2225–2241. https://doi.org/10.1007/s11423-021-09964-9

Stefaniak, J.E., & Xu, M. (2020). Leveraging dynamic decision-making and environmental analysis to support authentic learning in digital experiences. *Revista De Educacion a Distancia (RED), 60*(4). https://doi.org/10.6018/red.412171

Tessmer, M., & Wedman, J.F. (1990). A layers-of-necessity instructional development model. *Educational Technology Research and Development, 38*(2), 77–85. https://doi.org/10.1007/BF02298271

Van Dyke, J. (2005). Teaching choreography: Beginning with craft. *Journal of Dance Education, 5*(4), 116–124. https://doi.org/10.1080/15290824.2005.10387300

von Bertalanffy, L. (1968). *General systems theory* (Vol. 1). Braziller.

Wilson, M. (2002). Six views of embodied cognition. *Psychonomic Bulletin & Review, 9*(4), 625–636. https://doi.org/10.3758/BF03196322

Instructional Design as Communication

11

Insights From the Field of Journalism

Richard E. West

Rick's Story

I do not remember when we first knew. One of the exciting benefits of working in an active newsroom is you hear the news as soon as it breaks. A brief note on the Associated Press feed, perhaps, or a comment on a police scanner, or a tip called in. What I do remember was our city editor rushing back into the newsroom after already going home for the day and standing in the middle of the room, feverishly directing the chaos of swirling reporters like a skilled symphony conductor. Pointing and directing, he assigned reporters to cover different angles and guided page editors in how they should sculpt the front page. A big question was, what would our headline be for a story this massive? How would we design the front page for the biggest news in our lifetimes? In the end, the title of the front page was simply **"Miracles do Exist."**

What was the story? On March 12, 2003, Elizabeth Smart, 14 years old, had been kidnapped by knife point by Brian David Mitchell from her home in Salt Lake City, and now after nine months she had miraculously been found. Her story had certainly captured the state of Utah but had also enthralled the entire nation and world. She was assumed dead but had been found alive,

DOI: 10.4324/9781003268413-11

only 18 miles away from her home, dressed in white religious robes. It was truly the most amazing story any of us had worked on.

The feeling in the newsroom was electric. Everyone was engaged from every department of the newsroom. We knew we had to be at our best because this front page and these stories would be forever cemented in history. How people learned about and remembered Elizabeth's story would depend on how we told it over just the next couple of hours – a frighteningly small amount of time to tell a story of that magnitude.

But that was what made journalism such a fun career – the thrill, the adrenaline, the sense of urgency to tell people what they needed to know!

Fourteen months later, I walked away from my career as a journalist to begin a new one in learning and instructional design. I had spent the past six years working for several different daily newspapers in Utah and Idaho, beginning as a sports *stringer* reporting on high school teams and ending as a page editor for national and city news for *The Herald Journal* in Logan, Utah.

Walking away from the rush of the newsroom, I was keenly aware of how different a career as an instructional designer would be from that of a journalist. What I found surprising over the next few years, however, was how much these two disciplines have in common. At their core, both professions rely on storytelling because they understand how stories impact and motivate people to change, encourage retention of information, and manipulate perceptions. In addition, both professions recognize the delicate balance of media, communication, and information. Furthermore, both recognize this simple truth: at the end of the day, while the information conveyed is what matters most, how that information is packaged will determine what people do with that information.

In this chapter, I explore insights and strategies employed by journalists that can benefit instructional designers in their craft, including how journalists sequence information, quickly communicate them, and grab attention in an increasingly loud news market. I also discuss the importance of thoughtfully integrating multimedia to communicate, crafting accessible and engaging narratives, and interviewing firsthand sources from both sides of an issue to communicate the essence of an experience.

Sequencing Information in a World of Information Overload

Journalists are experts in communicating information concisely to inform readers and viewers of as many important stories in the quickest time possible. This is evidenced by their characteristic writing style – the inverted pyramid. Outside of journalism, information is often presented chronologically (this, then that), logically (there are X themes. . .), as point/counterpoint, or as a funnel from broad concepts to narrow ones (or vice versa, from narrow to broad).

For journalists, the structure is very different. First, a short *lede/lead* is written to immediately hook or grab the reader's attention. Next, the answers to the "5+ Ws" of who, what, where, when, why, (and how) is concisely presented in a sentence or two. For readers, this first paragraph provides the most important information, and often is the only part of the story shared in news summaries from around the world. If the rest of the story is given, it is presented in the format of an inverted pyramid, where information is presented in order of importance. Thus, the most important information is presented first, then the next important, and so on to the end (see Figure 11.1).

This style of writing was an innovation of late 19th century US journalism, and according to Pöttker (2003), developed as journalists focused on their readers, their needs, and how to best communicate with them. By World

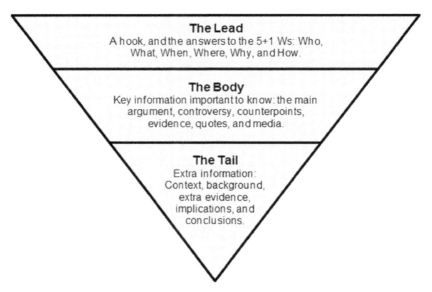

Figure 11.1 The inverted pyramid style of writing

War I, while European countries still presented information chronologically, American reports of the war largely followed the inverted pattern (Pöttker, 2003). Learning about the bullet that killed the archduke in the final sentence of the story, for example, proved to be a very poor way to learn about the Great War!

As a page editor, this style of writing was extremely helpful! My task was to grab stories off the Associated Press news feed and fit them into the spaces we had available on the page. If the story was too long, I did not need to read the story to make cuts. I simply cut from the bottom. This enabled me to fill a page of news very quickly when up against a deadline.

As paper news has increasingly converted to digital, the inverted pyramid style remains relevant. Now it is not page editors cutting stories, but rather readers who simply quit reading after a few paragraphs. Thus, it is still critical for journalists to give the most important information *above the fold*, or in modern times *above the scroll*.

This style of presenting information is quite different from how instructional designers often present information. For example, we might compare inverted pyramid style of information presentation to Gagne's (1965) events of instruction. Gagné argued that first we need to grab the learner's attention (similar to the journalistic lead), but that we then inform the reader of learning objectives and activate their prior knowledge – information that is arguably the least important because it is what the learner already knows. Content is then typically presented not in order of importance, but according to some logical sequence, often chronologically.

Certainly from a cognitive view of learning, it makes sense to activate schemas and present information in logical sequences. However, are there situations where instructional designers might benefit from an inverted pyramid method of presentation? We know that one of the most important factors in student learning is helping them stay engaged, particularly if they are adolescents (Borup et al., 2020).

If we know that engagement and attention are finite, we might need to humbly admit that the learners are not going to read all the information we provide them. Knowing this, there are many situations where we may need to think like journalists and provide learners with the 5+ Ws of the topic up front, and the most important lessons and information first, so that if, or rather when they drop out of the lesson, they have learned enough to meet the most critical objectives.

182 Richard E. West

PRACTICE ACTIVITY

Applying the Inverted Pyramid

Think about a lesson or module you are designing now. Write down the main topics or pieces of information, and then organize these by how important they are for the student to learn. Now consider whether it is possible to present the information in this order. What could you do to provide just enough context to understand each topic without burying the lead deep within the lesson? Can you put less essential information in a link for those interested in continuing their learning?

If you are a researcher in the field, try applying the inverted pyramid style to the abstract of your paper. Instead of writing chronologically (brief summary of the literature, summary of methods, summary of findings), write a single sentence at the beginning that answers the 5+ Ws of your paper, then follow up by writing the next most important information. Usually, this means the first line of your abstract will be the main finding of your paper. This method to writing abstracts is particularly useful because that first sentence will be the only sentence readers will see in internet searches and will be the reason they click to see your full paper.

Speaking to Users Through Multimedia

Prior to 1980, newspapers sold words, believing that the best words – creating the best and most concise stories – would sell papers. But in 1980, a different vision was created by mass media corporation Gannett when they created *USA TODAY* – a newspaper that was full color, innovative in its eye-popping front-page designs, and emphasized visual communication through charts, graphs, and images. In addition, the front page dedicated precious space not to telling the news, but in advertising stories found inside the paper (a feature called *reefers*).

The front page became the hook to entice readers walking past the newsstand, and it worked. Within three years, *USA TODAY* was the second-highest selling newspaper in the country. It is now the first. Besides its market success, *USA TODAY* became a design icon that journalists around the country tried to imitate. Joe Zeff, an interactive content designer, remarked, "Before there

Instructional Design as Communication   **183**

was an internet bursting with real-time news and Twitter feeds, there was *USA TODAY*. It was ESPN before there was ESPN and The Weather Channel before there was The Weather Channel. And it set a standard for young designers like myself" (García, 2012).

More recently, the lessons from *USA TODAY* – how blending multimedia and design with words can more effectively communicate and engage – has been critical to the survival of the journalism industry as it has shifted to the ruthless world of Internet media. Rather than being the "end of journalism" (Charles & Stewart, 2011), journalists have adapted by embracing media mogul Rupert Murdoch's insight that people were less likely to read newspapers or watch television news, but realizing instead that they would, in fact, still consume media (Sedorkin, 2020).

What has emerged is an industry that focuses on delivering ideas in as many different channels and methods as the public demands: paper, websites, television, podcasts, blogs, or even social media. In doing so, journalists have learned how to make the news more engaging through the use of multiple media channels (such as video or interactive simulations embedded with text) and more eye-catching through clever titles and web analytics. The concept of reefers from *USA TODAY* now exists in email and social media quick blasts that link readers to the full story.

In addition, many newsrooms quickly understood the need to consolidate all of their teams together under one mission of communicating information, whether they were technologists, writers, photographers, or managers. As an example, Sedorkin described the transformation of the newsroom of Australia's largest newspaper, *The Sydney Morning Herald*, to an integrated office where the key decision-makers from across the organization worked closely together in a central hub with the reporters, editorial staff, and content developers branching out as spokes. This meant that everyone creating, editing, producing, and pitching the news stories were within a few feet of each other – even across departments, such as the paper and web news teams. This kind of office interdisciplinary synergy became critical to the survival of many news organizations.

What are the lessons for instructional designers from journalism's increasing focus on integrating multimedia and multimedia experts on one team? I think there are several.

First, like news consumers are changing, the consumers of our instructional content are similarly changing. Our learners want content to be bite-sized but interconnected for deeper exploration. With the press on their attention from social media and mass media, instructional designers must be increasingly visual, exciting, and clickable to entice learners to engage with our content. Packaging our content in ways that appeal to the 21st century learner is not selling out, as some may worry, but instead selling the importance of the learning we are providing.

Second, we need to more fully embrace instructional multimedia. Despite understanding the role of media in coding information (Clark & Paivio, 1991) and the strategies for effectively using multimedia in learning (Mayer, 2005), instructional content is often surprisingly text-heavy. At our core, we seem to still believe instruction = content instead of instruction = experiences. Curriculum-writing is deep in our DNA, but we need to adapt and embrace teaching through a wide variety of media. Besides incorporating video and simulations as we have done recently, we can explore creative ways to mix media, through strategies such as *playable case studies* (Giboney et al., 2021) or "alternate reality" (Pellicone et al., 2016; Stretton et al., 2018).

Third, we need to fully embrace instructional design as a metafield (Bodily et al., 2019) that works collaboratively with professionals from many other domains to fully develop all the layers (Gibbons, 2013) of a learning experience. In our graduate programs, we need to teach in an interdisciplinary way, collaborating much more deeply with other departments so that our students experience the kind of integrated working that journalists at *The Sydney Morning Herald* did.

PRACTICE ACTIVITY

Designing a Landing Page

For a current project you are working on, take a step away from your wireframes and ask yourself:

- What writing could I replace with media? Will this media be supported by my learning management system?
- How could I mix media to create a richer experience (while adhering to ADA guidelines)?
- How could I interconnect pieces of content?

Try designing the landing page of your instruction to include reefers that refer to your other pieces of instruction. Can you make your landing page as exciting as *USA Today*? As Netflix? Could you use analytics to suggest to learners what they might want to learn about next?

Instructional Design as Communication **185**

In your own work and on your own team, could you be more collaborative and interdisciplinary? How could you increase the potential spillover of ideas from one group to another? Should you be combining your efforts more synergistically?

Tell Your Learners a Story

Previously, I described journalistic writing through the inverted pyramid style, which is efficient and effective at communicating the main ideas of a topic quickly, especially in hard news reports. However, sometimes a deeper dive is necessary, especially if the goal is to help learners understand an alternative perspective within the news. In these cases, journalists often involve narrative features common to fiction writers, in order to help readers reconstruct settings, chronology, and characters. This has the added benefit of helping readers develop empathy for the persons involved in the stories.

These longer, narrative-style pieces are often referred to as long-form journalism, narrative journalism, literary journalism, creative nonfiction, or feature news, and it was popularized in the mid-20th century by outlets such as the *New Yorker*, *Harpers*, *Reader's Digest*, and *The Atlantic*. Today these publications still exist, but are complemented by many others, as well as journalists sharing their narrative stories on blogs, medium, and in popular nonfiction books.

This narrative journalism retains classic elements of traditional journalism, such as a desire to reveal the truth of a situation, sourced information with spicy quotes, and a focus on informing the reader with clear takeaways. However, it adds to these principles the characteristics of good fiction, such as rich descriptions of a setting, detailed dialogue, strong characters, and action propelling the story forward on pivot points (Reagan, 2016).

In short, this style of journalism creates "true stories, well told" (see https://creativenonfiction.org/what-is-cnf/), which provides the benefit of deeply engaging a reader in understanding an issue or event. Besides a higher level of engagement with the topic, we understand from educational psychology that information is stored within our brains as connected schemas, and narrative provides a ready organization of information that makes learning, memorizing, and retaining information easier and with less cognitive load (Darejeh et al., 2021). Polkinghorne (1988) argued that narrative was essentially how

186 Richard E. West

humans "give meaning to their experience" and understand "the past events of one's life and (how to plan for) future actions. It is the primary scheme by means of which human existence is rendered meaningful" (p. 11).

It is for this reason that many researchers have argued for more narrative methods within learning and instructional design (Hokanson & Fraher, 2008). Jonassen and Hernandez-Serrano (2002) argued that stories are "a primary form of instructional support" for problem-based learning. This is because stories "are the most natural and powerful formalism for storing and describing experiential learning" (p. 65). Thus, helping learners to organize learning as stories, be able to retrieve these stories to reference with a new problem, and analyze the utility of various stories is an essential part of effective instruction.

One method to help learners develop these compelling, narrative structures in their brains is through actually designing learning experiences to have a narrative arc, much as is found in experience design (Matthews, 2018) and focusing more on the overall aesthetic experience in learning (Parrish, 2009). Indeed, Hokanson and Fraher (2008) argued that learners fit well the monomyth description of a hero's journey alongside a trusted mentor. One example may be the *DUST* mixed reality game created at Brigham Young University (Hollingshead, 2015). This instructional game was designed to teach middle school students neuroscience, biology, scientific method, and collaborative research skills. Table 11.1 provides a summary of the narrative of the game, using modified narrative structure elements from Labov and Waletzky (1997).

Table 11.1 Narrative Elements of the *DUST* Instructional Game

Story Element	Instructional Content/Topic
Who are the key characters?	Fictional middle schoolers on a tour of a NASA museum, who realize the world is suffering a crisis that needs their help. Real-world students playing the game join the fictional characters in solving the crisis.
What are the characters' relationships?	Fictional characters have access to NASA instruments and data, while real-world learners are attending school together.

(Continued)

Instructional Design as Communication **187**

Table 11.1 (Continued)

Story Element	Instructional Content/Topic
What is the abstract that summarizes the story and hooks the learner?	After a meteor flashes across the sky, spewing cosmic dust, adults fall to the ground in a coma. Only the youth are still alive and must answer the following questions: "What is happening, and why is it only affecting adults?" (see promotional video at https://bit.ly/DustVideo).
How can we orient the learner to the story? Who/what is involved, and when/where?	Real-world students participate by first watching the promotional video, and then reading graphic novel-style information that orients them to the fictional characters in the NASA lab.
What is the complicating action or crisis?	The meteor, as well as data shared on social media of parents/adults being affected locally (in the game, students can download an app to scan people, and when it gives an infected rating, they upload the data to the game to share with others. This data helps uncover the mystery that only adults are infected).
What is the resolution, and how did it emerge?	Over a couple of weeks, information and clues from the fictional characters working inside of NASA are given. Student game players use these clues and formulate scientific hypotheses to test against new data. The game leads players to discover the cause of the virus and the solution.
What is the evaluation/explanation that helps us learn "so what?"	Beyond learning the answer to the virus, students learn about how to engage in a scientific process with data to find answers.
How can the learner transform the narrative events/lessons to their own situation?	By seeing youths like themselves working with NASA to resolve the crisis, they see their potential futures as scientists.
What is the Coda, or wrap-up and final lesson learned?	Science and the scientific method is a strong method for resolving real-world problems.

188 Richard E. West

Regardless of whether the story in our instructional design is a narrative that the learner experiences themselves, as the students did in this *Falling DUST* game, or if we simply use more stories to communicate our content in more traditional ways, employing these narrative strategies will promote higher engagement, greater empathy, and deeper understanding from our learners.

PRACTICE ACTIVITY

Exploring Story Elements

After completing a storyboard or content/task analysis for a learning experience, consider how to organize the content through narrative by filling out the following table with your own content, adapted from Labov and Waletzky's (1997) approach to narrative qualitative analysis:

Story Element	Instructional Content/Topic
Who are the key characters?	
What are the characters' relationships with each other?	
What is the abstract that summarizes the story and hooks the learner?	
How can we orient the learner to the story? Who/what is involved and when/where?	
What is the complicating action or crisis?	
What is the resolution, and how did it emerge?	
What is the evaluation/explanation that helps us learn "so what?"	
How can the learner transform the narrative events/lessons to their own situation?	
What is the Coda or wrap-up and final lesson learned?	

Source Information Through Interviewing

Perhaps the most ubiquitous and recognizable image of a journalist is that of a reporter with a recorder asking questions and taking notes on a 4-inch-wide Portage notebook (the classic, fits-in-your-hand notebook reporters have used for generations). In other words, the classic journalistic interview.

Interviewing is of course a key skill for designers of learning and instruction as well. Interviews are used to collect information about potential learners, and to evaluate the effectiveness of instructional products. When designers become researchers (such as in design-based research; see Christensen & West, 2018), interviewing becomes a key method for collecting data.

Interviewing methods currently in vogue in learning and instructional design derive primarily from the psychological interviewing method (e.g., Kvale, 2012), or ethnographic methods (Spradley, 2016). Journalistic interviewing strategies are similar, but diverge slightly in intention, method, and use. For reporters, the key principles for effective interviewing are as follows:

Prepare

Come to the interview having already immersed yourself in the topic. This allows you to meet the interviewee at a higher plane of understanding, convey trust that you can interpret their words correctly, and help you ask more informed questions.

Use Questions to Match the Interview Purpose

Journalists primarily conduct interviews either to learn information or to profile a person or situation. The former focuses on the 5+ Ws (who, what, when, where, why, and how) of the situation. Similar to the inverted pyramid style of writing, journalists ask the most important questions first because sometimes one or two questions is all you will get as you interview a cop by the scene of a crime or a politician in a news conference. If time permits, after gathering the basic facts, you can return to previous questions to ask for follow-up information and detail. Meanwhile, in a feature or profile interview, the purpose is to deeply understand the person or event and what makes them unique. The focus is also on creating description and narrative, and thus

190 Richard E. West

questions ask about what was heard, seen, felt, or experienced, in addition to how the event was understood or interpreted by the person.

Be Objective

Journalism ethics traditionally has emphasized reporting the news objectively. As journalistic scholars have realized that objectivity is often impossible, they have instead emphasized having balance and fairness in reporting. Regardless, the focus of the interview should be on setting aside one's own biases and perceptions and seeking to understand the facts as they are possible to know and the feelings of the people experiencing the event.

Grab the Quotes

Journalists are particularly skilled at recognizing a good quote within a long, rambling response. This skill is often mocked, as journalists are often blamed (sometimes with good reason) for reporting a single quote out of context. However, this nose for a quote can be a good and useful, tactic, as journalists can be very skilled at finding the statement that best summarizes what the person was trying to say and represents their experience in the fewest words possible. When the reporter follows good ethical practice of checking their notes with the interviewee and distancing their own biases from the report, their ability to use lively quotes can help readers feel empathy and engagement for the story.

Source All Facts From Both Sides

An important ethical practice for journalists is to not report any information without verifying it with key sources (usually multiple sources). Part of this is finding sources from both sides of an issue to present a balanced report.

Skeptical readers of this chapter may argue that some modern journalists stray from many of these ethical practices. I argue that similarly there are scientific researchers or instructional designers that do not adhere to the top ethical practices of their disciplines! Despite this, the foundational principles of journalistic interviewing can be useful for learning and instructional designers. First, like journalists, we should approach our interviews with subject matter experts having already done our homework in that content area so that we can have productive discussions. Second, it is important to remember what our purpose is for each interview. In a user experience interview, we want to understand the facts, without bias or influence, about how the user experiences the product and where the errors in the system are. In creating learner personas (Fulgencio & Asino, 2021), we need to be able to explain and describe vividly the kinds of user groups there are and what kinds of people they are.

There are lessons for us in design research as well. For example, journalists can teach us the importance of sourcing all of our ideas from both sides, using "negative case analysis" (Williams, 2018) to check our biases by looking for data both for and against an idea. Like journalists, an effective strategy in reporting qualitative data is to use in vivo quotes (Manning, 2017) that reflect the color and key ideas in a person's response. These lively quotes cannot only help communicate ideas in a research report but can be more persuasive to stakeholders in an evaluation report and help them understand and empathize.

PRACTICE ACTIVITY

Develop Your Interviewing Skills

Practice each of the following journalistic interviewing skills by completing the following activities for a user or learner interview.

Preparation: Write up a one-page crib sheet of the main ideas in the area of the person that you are interviewing. Consider the purpose of the interview – is it to find information or to profile a person or event? Develop questions to match your purpose, either to get quickly to the most important information or to create a profile of the event. For informational interviews, rely on the 5+ Ws and ask open-ended questions. For profile interviews, consider beginning the interview by creating the context or scene, asking participants questions like "Describe for me what this experience was like?" or "Explain to me as if someone was experiencing this for the first time." If it is helpful to know the story and how it unfolded, ask chronology questions like "Tell me step-by-step what happened?"

Source both sides objectively. Before beginning, consider what biases you may bring to this experience. Write down a paragraph or two that

> describes your position about the issue before the interview begins. Later, you can check your findings and conclusions against your initial position statement and, if necessary, collect additional data to test against your original assumptions (e.g., negative case analysis).
>
> Look for the quotes! While interviewing, star or mark the quotes that seem especially salient. In analyzing your data later, create in vivo codes that utilize the participants' own words. In writing up your report, look for a prototypical quote that best represents the color and emotion the participants felt about that issue.

Conclusion: Evolving Worlds of Journalism and Design

In this chapter, I have reviewed several key principles and strategies used by journalists to execute their craft, and drawn comparisons and lessons learned for how these strategies can benefit designers of learning and instruction. Perhaps the strongest lesson we can learn from journalism, however, is adaptability. In 2003, when I turned in my last byline to *The Herald Journal* in Logan, Utah, it was clear that the field of journalism was changing rapidly. The Internet was quickly increasing the amount of information available to journalists. Even more disruptive was that it was rapidly changing the amount of information available directly to readers. If journalists were going to remain the providers of news and stories, they would have to evolve.

And evolve they have, consolidating newsrooms into multimedia production studios, cross training storytellers so that they can tell their stories in multiple mediums, and growing into a 24-hour, always on, social media news cycle. Through it all, several key lessons have remained true for journalists:

Having ideas is important. Knowing how to communicate these ideas might be more important. Interesting information, packaged in a dull and boring wrapping, will not get read, shared, or learned.

When time is short, share the most important information first.

Stories are the essence of life. They are how we learn, how we experience the world, and how we remember. Information told through stories communicates to what is human within all of us.

Information needs to be well-sourced from both sides of an issue. Personal interviews help us understand the essence of the news or of an experience.

These lessons have relevance for learning and instructional designers as well, particularly the lesson of adaptability. As the world continues to

Instructional Design as Communication **193**

evolve, how learners experience education will change as well. The future world of instructional design might be more micro and stackable (West & Cheng, 2022), more open and shareable (Wiley, 2018), more informal as well as formal (Boileau, 2018), and more focused on design skill rather than design process (McDonald & West, 2021). Through the evolving changes, however, key principles and concepts will remain true. One such principle is the importance of focusing on the human experience, above and beyond simply sharing content. As Lord Alfred Harmsworth, legendary British news publisher said, "It is hard news that catches readers. Features hold them." In other words, content may bring in learners to our instruction, but developing empathy, deep understanding, and human connection will retain them.

Reference List

Bodily, R., Leary, H., & West, R.E. (2019). Research trends in instructional design and technology journals. *British Journal of Educational Technology*, *50*(1), 64–79.

Boileau, T. (2018). Informal learning. In R. West (Ed.), *Foundations of learning and instructional design technology*. https://edtechbooks.org/lidtfoundations/informal_learning

Borup, J., Graham, C.R., West, R.E., Archambault, L., & Spring, K.J. (2020). Academic Communities of Engagement: An expansive lens for examining support structures in blended and online learning. *Educational Technology Research and Development*, *68*(2), 807–832.

Charles, A., & Stewart, G.A. (2011). *The end of journalism: News in the twenty-first century*. Peter Lang.

Christensen, K., & West, R.E. (2018). The development of design-based research. In R. West (Ed.), *Foundations of learning and instructional design technology*. https://edtechbooks.org/lidtfoundations/development_of_design-based_research/simple

Clark, J.M., & Paivio, A. (1991). Dual coding theory and education. *Educational Psychology Review*, *3*(3), 149–210.

Darejeh, A., Marcus, N., & Sweller, J. (2021). The effect of narrative-based E-learning systems on novice users' cognitive load while learning software applications. *Educational Technology Research and Development*, *69*(5), 2451–2473.

Fulgencio, J., & Asino, T.I. (2021). Conducting a learner analysis. In J.K. McDonald & R.E. West (Eds.), *Design for learning*. https://edtechbooks.org/id/learner_analysis

Gagné, R.M. (1965). *The conditions of learning*. Holt, Rinehart & Winston.

García, M.R. (2012, September 9). *USA TODAY turns 30: Part 1*. García Media.

Gibbons, A.S. (2013). *An architectural approach to instructional design*. Routledge.

Giboney, J.S., McDonald, J.K., Balzotti, J., Hansen, D.L., Winters, D.M., & Bonsignore, E. (2021). Increasing cybersecurity career interest through playable case studies. *TechTrends*, *65*(4), 496–510.

Hokanson, B., & Fraher, R. (2008). Narrative structure, myth, and cognition for instructional design. *Educational Technology*, *48*, 27–32.

Hollingshead, T. (2015, January 20). BYU'S new alternate reality game: Save your parents' lives with science. *BYU University Communications News*. https://news.byu.edu/news/byus-new-alternate-reality-game-save-your-parents-lives-science

Jonassen, D.H., & Hernandez-Serrano, J. (2002). Case-based reasoning and instructional design: Using stories to support problem solving. *Educational Technology Research and Development, 50*(2), 65–77.

Kvale, S. (2012). *Doing interviews*. Sage.

Labov, W., & Waletzky, J. (1997). Narrative analysis: Oral versions of personal experience. *Journal of Narrative & Life History, 7*(1–4), 3–38. https://doi.org/10.1075/jnlh.7.02nar

Manning, J. (2017). In vivo coding. *The International Encyclopedia of Communication Research Methods, 24*, 1–2.

Matthews, M.T. (2018). Designing for narrative-like learning experiences. In *Educational technology and narrative* (pp. 249–258). Springer.

Mayer, R.E. (Ed.). (2005). *The Cambridge handbook of multimedia learning*. Cambridge University Press.

McDonald, J.K., & West, R.E. (2021). *Design for learning: Principles, processes, and praxis*. https://edtechbooks.org/id

Parrish, P.E. (2009). Aesthetic principles for instructional design. *Educational Technology Research and Development, 57*(4), 511–528. http://www.jstor.org/stable/40388645

Pellicone, A., Bonsignore, E., Ahn, J., Kaczmarek, K., Hansen, D., & Kraus, K. (2016). *The social shape of dust: Learning networks in alternate reality games*. Proceedings of International Conference.

Polkinghorne, D.E. (1988). *Narrative knowing and the human sciences*. State University of New York.

Pöttker, H. (2003). News and its communicative quality: The inverted pyramid – when and why did it appear? *Journalism Studies, 4*(4), 501–511.

Reagan, M. (2016, December 6). Conventions of literary journalism. *Medium*. https://medium.com/duluth-immersion-journal/conventions-of-literary-journalism-f57fd723792f

Sedorkin, G. (2020). *Reporting in a multimedia world: An introduction to core journalism skills*. Routledge.

Spradley, J.P. (2016). *The ethnographic interview*. Waveland Press.

Stretton, T., Cochrane, T., & Narayan, V. (2018). Exploring mobile mixed reality in healthcare higher education: A systematic review. *Research in Learning Technology, 26*, 2131–2131.

West, R.E., & Cheng, Z. (2022). Digital credential evolution: How open microcredentials/badges support learning in micro, meso, and macro levels. In O. Zawacki-Richter & I. Jung (Eds.), *Handbook of open, distance, and digital education*. Sage.

Wiley, D. (2018). Open educational resources. In R. West (Ed.), *Foundations of learning and instructional design technology*. https://edtechbooks.org/lidtfoundations/open_educational_resources

Williams, D.D. (2018). *Qualitative inquiry in daily life*. https://edtechbooks.org/qualitative inquiry

Index

ABC story game 115
academia 37–38
accountability 47–48
acting 103–104
active listening 117–118, 155
ADDIE (analysis, design, development, implementation, evaluation) 18–19
agency 64
Alcoff, Linda 59
Andrews, Gavin J. 133
Aristotle 72
assessment: hazard 88–94; levels of understanding 81–82; risk 88–94, 99–100
Association for Talent Development (ATD) 16, 28
attitudes domain 6
audience considerations 70–71

Baaki, John 57
Bardzell, Shaowen 62
Bloom, Benjamin 6
Bloom's revised taxonomy 79–80
book clubs 146
brainstorming 108, 111–113
Branch, Robert M. 4
Briggs, Leslie 5
buy-in 43, 67–68, 71, 73, 82

Carr, Alison A. 56
carrier bag metaphor 52–53, 55
Carry Bag of Theory of Fiction, The (Le Guin) 51

Cennamo, Kathy 7
change management 12–13
character development 113–114
Christmas Carol, A (Dickens) 103
Churchill, Winston 42, 48
Clements, Jim 11
client management 17–22
cognitive strategies domain 6
collaboration: acting 104; instructional designers 107–111; in STEM 154–156; strategies for enhancing 107–113; unexpected scenarios 106
collaborative cartoon game 109–110
Collins, Damian 138
communication: journalism 179–182; multimedia 182–185, 192; risk communication 97–98; strategies for better 117–119
complexity 92
composure 108
concept translation 19–22
Conditions of Learning (Gagné) 6
consultation: mindset 22–28; project management 12
context 64
course assets. 89
course delivery 101
course design 57, 71, 85
course development 100
course template 95
COVID-19 pandemic 129–130
Crenshaw, Kimberlé W. 56–57

196 Index

crisis management 84
criterion-referenced testing 6
critical learning 78
critical race theory 56
critical theories 53–55
critical thinking 151–154
culture 52

dance choreography 165–166, 171–175
dance education 159–160
Data Feminism (D'Ignazio and Klein) 55, 63
decision-making 168–169
Deming Cycle Plan 84, 86
Department of Homeland Security
   (DHS) 86
design flow 169–171
design justice 55
Dewey, John 46
Dickens, Charles 103
D'Ignazio, Catherine 56, 63
DiPietro, Eddie 36
Disability Visibility Project (DVP) 62
diversity 147, 156
documentation: hazard impact 85–86, 94;
   resilience plan 97
Doyle, Arthur Conan 120
DUST mixed reality game 186–188
dynamic decision-making 168–169
dynamic systems 162–165

embodiment 55, 61–63
emotion 61, 64, 72, 73, 192
empathy 68–69, 76
equity 147, 156
ESPN 183
ethics 54, 55, 56, 64
ethos 71, 73
everyday object 122
expectations 155

Facebook 147
Faigley, Lester 70
failure 149
feedback 74–76, 171
feminist theory: embodiment 55, 61–62;
   impact on instructional design practice
   56; incorporating into instructional
   design practice 63–64; intersectionality
   55; positionality 55, 58–60; reflexivity
   55, 58–60; role 55
Fisher, Elizabeth 52

five questions game 115
five things 122
Flanagan, John 5
flow 169–174
follow-up 146
Freire, Paulo 59
Freund, Jack 86

Gagné, Robert 5, 6, 181
Gesler, Wilbert 128, 133
Gibbs' Reflective Cycle 74–76
Gido, Jack 11
gifts game 109
Glasser, Robert 6
goals 149, 171
Good Reasons with Contemporary Arguments
   (Faigley and Selzer) 70
gratitude 150
group work 95

Harmsworth, Alfred 193
hazard assessment 88–94
hazard controls 85, 94–96, 98
hazard identification 86–88
hazard impact 85–86, 94, 95–96
health 137–138
health geography 132, 137–138
Hernandez-Serrano, Julian 186
Holmes, Sherlock 120–121
hooks, b. 140
HPT movement 6
human-computer interaction design
   (HCI) 55
human performance technology 4
Hybrid Pedagogy (journal) 54

identity 143–144
identity-centered design 57h
impact scoring 90–92
inclusion 147, 156
inclusive teaching 57, 65
independent thinking 144–147
inexperienced subject matter expert
   150–151, 153–154, 157
infomercial game 115
innovation 37, 40–42, 45, 46
instructional designers (IDs):
   accountability 47–48; buy-in 43;
   collaboration 107–111; communication
   116–119; consultation 12; culture
   45; demonstration 44–45; goals

Index **197**

9–10; growth mindset 42–49; project management 11–12; reflection 46–47; role 3, 11, 54–55; skill set 2–3, 9–11, 13, 48–49; tasks 1–2; unexpected scenarios 106, 116, 119–120; value 13; vision 43–44

instructional design (ID): applying STEM identity 144; applying STEM identity to 144; audience considerations 70–71; choreography of 160–161, 171–175; client management 17–22; collaboration 154–155; core tenets 7; critical thinking 151–152; definitions 3–7, 63, 160–161; embryonic systems view, 8; feminist approaches 51–64; hazard controls 94–96; historical context in US 5–7; independent thinking 145; instructional systems design view 8–9; knowledge base. 4; lessons from language instruction 67–82; mapping projects 166–168, 172–173; marketing strategies 15–34; media view 7–8; mindset 8; misconceptions 7–9; multimedia 183–185, 192; principles for feminist 55, 63–64; principles of feminist 55–56; problem-solving 151–152; self-regulating systems 168; solution creation 17–22; story telling 185–188; as system 162–165; value 2

Instructional Design Knowledge Base, The (Richey) 162

intellectual skills domain 6

interaction 146

International Board of Standards for Training, Performance and Instruction (IBSTPI) 4

International Society for Performance Improvement (ISPS) 4

intersectionality 55, 56–58

interrupted story conversation 122

interviews 189–192

inverted pyramid 179–182

Jefferson, Thomas 36

Jen, Natasha 58

Jonassen, David H. 56, 186

Jones, Jack 86

journalism: multimedia 183–185, 192; story telling 178–179, 185–188; writing style 179–182

Kalk, Debby 7

Kazanas, H. 4

Kearns, Robin A. 132–133, 138

Klein, Lauren F. 56, 63

knowledge management 6

landing page 184–185

language instruction: buy-in 68–69; college ESL classroom 76–82; college writing classroom 70–76; empathy 68–69; instructional design lessons 67–82

learner agency 56

learner and task analysis 6

learner-centered pedagogy 78–80

learners 68–69, 77, 79–80, 123–124, 136, 139, 181, 183, 185–188

learning 2–3, 6, 12–13, 58, 65, 69, 77–78, 80–82, 181

learning designers 100–101

learning environments 136

learning scientists 7

Le Guin, Ursula K. 51–52, 61–62, 65

"Lessons From the Barre" (Stefaniak) 9

likelihood scoring 90

LinkedIn 147

Litzinger, Mary Ellen 56

logos 71–72, 73

Mager, Robert 6

mapping 166–168, 172–173

marketing strategies 15–17

Marks, Howard 40

Marra, Rose M. 56

Mead, George Herbert 143

Measuring and Managing Information Risk (Freund and Jones) 86

memory 72

military organization 37–38

Mind, Self, and Society from the Standpoint of a Social Behaviorist (Mead) 143

multimedia 182–185, 192

narrative journalism 185–188

NASA Aerospace Education Services Project 83

National Institute of Standards and Technology (NIST) 86

negative case analysis 191

note-taking 145–146

198 Index

Oaktree Capital Management 40
objectivity 190
one-minute persona game 115
one word story game 118
On Rhetoric (Aristotle) 72
opportunity 38–40, 43
outside perspective 46–47

pathos 72, 73
pausing 145
performance standards 42
Pillow, Wanda 59
place: conceptualization 132–133;
    as relational 135–136; as social
    construction 133–134
pluralism 64
points of view 117
political work 54, 65
positionality 55, 58–60
positivity 108
Pöttker, Horst 180
power 55, 65
praxis 59
*Principles of Risk Analysis: Decision Making
    under Uncertainty* (Yoe) 86
problem identification 27
problem-solving: skills 120; in STEM
    151–154; strategies for 120–124
programmed instruction 5–6
project-based learning 80–82
project management 11–12
Project Management Institute
    (PMI) 86
psychomotor skills domain 6

quality assurance tools 41
Quality Matters quality assurance
    tools 41
questions only game 118–119
quotes 190, 191

reflection 46, 74–76
reflective learning 78
reflexivity 55, 58–60
Reiser, Robert A. 4, 5
relational geography 135–137
resilience 148; *see also* risk resilience
revision 74–76
rhetoric 72
rhetorical appeals 71–73
Richey, Rita C. 4, 160, 162

risk: aversion 40–42, 43; definitions 37–38;
    growth mindset 42–49; hazard controls
    94–96; myths 39; opportunity 38–40,
    43; rewards 36; scenarios 89–90; score
    table 93
risk assessment 88–94, 99–100
risk communication 97–98
risk resilience: definitions 85–86; five-step
    methodology for plan 86–102; hazard
    assessment 88–94, 99–100; hazard
    controls 85, 94–96, 98; hazard d 97;
    hazard identification 86–88; hazard
    impact documentation 85–86, 94; risk
    communication 97–98
risk-taking: academia 37–38; military
    organization 37–38
Robinson, Kate 35
Robinson, Ken 35
role play game 119
Rothwell, William J. 4

Sagan, Carl 42
Schiffman, Shirl S. 8
science, technology, engineering, and
    mathematics (STEM): applying
    identity to instructional design
    144; collaboration 154–156; critical
    thinking 151–154; problem-solving
    151–154; resilience and perseverance in
    148–151; scenarios 156–157; thinking
    independently 144
Sedorkin, Gail 183
self-regulating instructional design
    systems 168
Selzer, Jack 70
siloed subject matter expert 155–156, 157
Skinner, B.F. 5
small chances 150
SMART goals 149
social media 147, 183
solution creation 17–28
solutions 121
space management 165–166
Stefaniak, Jill E. 9, 57
story telling 185–188
storytelling 174–175
strategic profile development 23–27
Strommel, Jesse 54
subject matter expert (SME) 1, 8, 11, 13,
    43, 46, 71, 105, 106, 111, 116, 119–120,
    123–124, 153–154, 155–156, 157

success: measures 31–33; questions for 38
SUNY OSCQR rubric 41
systems 162–165, 174–175
systems thinking 8–9

television production 104–105
TESOL (Teaching English to Speakers of Other Languages) 69, 76–78, 82
therapeutic landscapes 128–132
Thiel, Peter 38
trust 104, 106, 113–117
Twitter 147
Tyler, Ralph 6

understanding 81–82
USA TODAY 182–183

verbal information domain 6
vision 107–108
visual cues 152
vulnerability 114–115

walking away 152
Weather Channel 183
well-being 139
Willis Towers Watson (WTW) 45
Wong, Alice 62

"Yes, and . . ." game 110–111
Yoe, Charles 86

Zeff, Joe 182
Zuckerberg, Mark 38

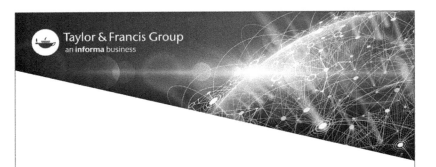

Taylor & Francis eBooks

www.taylorfrancis.com

A single destination for eBooks from Taylor & Francis with increased functionality and an improved user experience to meet the needs of our customers.

90,000+ eBooks of award-winning academic content in Humanities, Social Science, Science, Technology, Engineering, and Medical written by a global network of editors and authors.

TAYLOR & FRANCIS EBOOKS OFFERS:

- A streamlined experience for our library customers
- A single point of discovery for all of our eBook content
- Improved search and discovery of content at both book and chapter level

REQUEST A FREE TRIAL
support@taylorfrancis.com

Milton Keynes UK
Ingram Content Group UK Ltd.
UKHW021622041224
451949UK00025B/455